WINNING WITH OPTIONS

WINNING WITH OPTIONS

The Smart Way to Manage Portfolio Risk
and Maximize Profit

MICHAEL C. THOMSETT

AMACOM

American Management Association

New York • Atlanta • Brussels • Chicago • Mexico City • San Francisco
Shanghai • Tokyo • Toronto • Washington, D.C.

Special discounts on bulk quantities of AMACOM books are available to corporations, professional associations, and other organizations. For details, contact Special Sales Department, AMACOM, a division of American Management Association, 1601 Broadway, New York, NY 10019.
Tel: 212-903-8316. Fax: 212-903-8083.
E-mail: specialsls@amanet.org
Website: www.amacombooks.org/go/specialsales
To view all AMACOM titles go to: www.amacombooks.org

This publication is designed to provide accurate and authoritative information in regard to the subject matter covered. It is sold with the understanding that the publisher is not engaged in rendering legal, accounting, or other professional service. If legal advice or other expert assistance is required, the services of a competent professional person should be sought.

Library of Congress Cataloging-in-Publication Data

Thomsett, Michael C.
    Winning with options : the smart way to manage portfolio risk and maximize profit / Michael C. Thomsett.
        p.   cm.
    Includes index.
    ISBN 978-0-8144-0033-3 (pbk.)
    1. Stock options.   2. Options (Finance)   3. Portfolio management.   I. Title.

    HG6042.T466   2008
    332.63'2283—dc22

                                                                    2007039114

Printing number

10   9   8   7   6   5   4   3   2   1

CONTENTS

Chapter 10

WINNING WITH OPTIONS

PORTFOLIO MANAGEMENT ALTERNATIVES

"Civilization and profits go hand in hand."
—Calvin Coolidge, November 27, 1920

MOST INVESTORS FACE a series of dilemmas in the course of managing their portfolio. When a stock's value rises, do you sell and take your profit? When value falls, do you cut your losses? Or do you ignore short-term price gyrations and hold for the long term?

No one solution is right for everyone. But if you want to hold stocks over a period of many months or even years, there are ways you can take profits or protect against downside movement without selling stock. The solution involves the smart and safe use of options—intangible rights attached to specific stocks.

Options are complex financial instruments. They are intangible, have a limited lifetime, and are confusing as the result of the industry's own specialized lingo. All of this can be troubling if you do not thoroughly understand how options can be used.

1

Options are often viewed as appropriate only for individuals who are willing to assume extraordinary risks. The truth is quite different, however:

- Options *can* be high-risk, but they can also be exceptionally conservative, depending on which strategies you use.

- Properly used, options can provide you with current income and very little market risk, even if you are a long-term "hold" investor.

- When you want to buy options, you can protect yourself by making a "contingent purchase" instead of an outright purchase. This alternative makes sense. It enables you to buy only if and when the value of the stock rises, but at a fixed price (and available up to nearly three years from entry into the position). The strategy also creates immediate cash flow, which provides you with downside protection.

When dealing with your portfolio, you have probably looked into various possibilities. You might have considered buying index funds or ETFs (Exchange-Traded Funds) because you don't know how else to manage the up and down movements in your portfolio and because you are concerned with immediate market risk. That is a mistake. Buying such spectrum investments cannot ever beat the market; they are more likely to duplicate market-wide performance or even result in performance below market averages. To really achieve a better return, you need to figure out how to arrive at a sensible, safe, and effective method to protect your stock positions while producing extra cash flow. This is where sensible application of options comes into the picture.

Options can be used:

- *To ensure a profitable position in a stock without needing to take profits.* Using long puts, you can guarantee that if the stock goes down, you will keep your profits.

- *In a "contingent purchase" strategy.* Under the right circumstances, this strategy increases current yield with little added risk and is smarter than buying additional shares of stock.

- *To actually take profits using covered calls while keeping the stock and dividends.* The covered call is a cash cow for stockholders and can be used to take current yield up into double digits with no added market risk. This is a safe and conservative strategy.

- *To leverage relatively small amounts of capital, limiting risk.* Buying long-term options sets the price, so that you can decide to: (1) take no action because the stock did not go up, (2) sell the option at a profit, or (3) exercise the option and buy 100 shares of stock at a price far below current market value. Maximum risk is limited to the price of the option.

- *To control stock for up to three years without purchasing it.* The alternative is to buy 100 shares of stock, but with options you can keep the possibility open while risking very little capital.

- *To effectively play both sides of swing trading and day trading strategies, without ever having to go short.* Short-term traders using only stock have to take extraordinary risks when selling short to play both sides, or to reduce risks by only acting on buy signals. Options solve this problem while enabling short-term traders to vastly expand their trading portfolio, since options cost much less than stock.

This book explains all of these strategies for portfolio management, including explanations of option terminology, market risks, and the mechanics of trades. One of the most important analytical steps you need to learn how to master is risk assessment of stock holdings. Options provide you with a means for reducing or eliminating risk without having to expose capital or sell stock you would rather keep. If you are willing to master a few basic rules and study a few strategies, you will discover that options are powerful portfolio management tools. They can be used not only to produce extra income but also to protect your long-term positions.

A FEW BASICS

One of the greatest pieces of economic wisdom is to know what you do not know.

—John Kenneth Galbraith, in *Time Magazine*, March 3, 1961

MAGINE INVESTING IN A COMPANY, holding shares of stock for the long term while earning a nice dividend each year, and watching your portfolio grow over time in a robust and healthy economy. Now imagine expanding this idea to create *additional* benefits. These include being able to take profits when they occur as a result of short-term overreaction in the market, to protect your stock against price declines, and to *use* your shares of stock to increase current income each and every year—when the stock rises and when it falls.

That environment does exist. With the careful, well-planned use of options, you can manage your portfolio to reduce overall risk while increasing current income. At the same time, you can satisfy the urge to speculate without placing your long-term investments at risk. You might not think of yourself as a risk taker, but most people like to imagine what it would be like to play short-term price movement and make a little extra money doing so. If you are typical, you probably have not gone down that road because you do not want to place your investment capital at risk, and that is a legitimate reason to play it safe. However, this book lays out a series of strategies involving options that you can use to create the ideal stock environment without added risk. Options are flexible and present many great opportunities, making them a practical income generator and risk-reducing device.

Ground Rules for Stock Selection

You have probably heard about options in terms of high risk and high loss. They are often seen as speculative "side bets" that only the high rolling risk taker wants to use. But this is not necessarily the case. A large number of option strategies are actually low-risk and worth considering even in the most conservative portfolio.

   To establish a clear definition of options and how they work, you need to be aware that an option is merely a "right." It has no tangible value and only grants its owner the ability to transact stock at a predetermined price. This gets interesting when the stock price moves above or below that set price. The more the movement of the price, the more valuable the option becomes—because the option fixes the price of the stock, no matter what its market price is at the time.

   To understand this in a way familiar to many people, consider the case of a real estate lease-option contract. Under this deal, a person who wants to buy a home enters into a lease with the owner, agreeing to pay a specified amount of rent for a period of years. In addition, the contract specifies that at any time before expiration of the lease, the tenant also has the right (the "option") to buy the house at a specified, fixed amount. Therefore, even if the market value of the home doubles, the tenant has the contractual right to exercise the option and buy the house. Numerous possible outcomes can occur, as shown in the example below.

EXAMPLE

You want to buy a house currently valued at $265,000 but you do not have the down payment. You believe that you can save up enough to buy the house within three years, so you offer the owner a lease-option. It specifies that you will make lease payments over a 36-month period, and also that at any time you can exercise an option to buy the house for $265,000. At the end of the lease term, the option expires. Several outcomes may occur:

- You are unable to save enough, or the house actually declines in market value. You allow the lease to expire without taking any action.

- The house doubles in value to more than $500,000 and you exercise the option. The owner is required by contract to sell the house to you for $265,000.

- The property increases in value and the owner does not want to sell, so he offers to buy your option from you. The price is negotiated based on current market value versus the option value of the property.

The kind of real estate transaction shown in this example occurs quite often. Now apply the same concept to the stock market and you have a fairly good idea of how it all works. For the price you pay to buy an option, you fix the price of stock. A *call* option gives you the right (but not the obligation) to buy 100 shares of a specific stock, on or before a specified deadline (the *expiration date*), for an exact price (the *strike price*). The opposite is a *put*, which is an option granting its owner the right to sell 100 shares of stock on or before expiration and at a specific strike price. For option sellers, the rights are ceded to buyers. The rules for both types of options are summarized in Figure 1-1.

Before jumping in and starting to buy (or to sell) calls and puts—or before investing in stock with option trading in mind—you need to consider the risk elements, not only of options but also within your stock portfolio. As a starting point, a series of commonsense rules will help you to keep your stock portfolio and options in perspective. First is the "rule" that your long-term portfolio objectives should govern all of your decisions:

Rule #1: Pick stocks based on your well-defined objectives and risk tolerance levels, and never based on potential gains from options. Too many first-time option investors make the mistake of picking stocks based on the value of related options. Another mistake is keeping high-risk stocks in your portfolio because options are poten-

FIGURE 1-1. COMPARISONS BETWEEN CALLS AND PUTS.

	CALL	PUT
THE BUYER	has a right but not an obligation to:	
	buy 100 shares at a fixed price	sell 100 shares at a fixed price
THE SELLER	may be required to:	
	sell 100 shares at a fixed price	buy 100 shares at a fixed price

tially profitable, when you would otherwise sell and replace those shares with safer stocks.

Rule #2: Be sure the stocks you hold are appropriate for you, and when that is no longer true, sell and replace those shares.

The third rule to remember is related to the long-term nature of most portfolios.

Rule #3: Select stocks based on your belief about long-term price appreciation, above all other considerations.

This final rule is the basic "value investing" approach. Under this premise, any long-term hold stocks should be in highly-valued, well-managed, competitively dominant companies whose stock you can buy at a bargain price (and then hold for the long term). Although this premise makes sense, it does not preclude options. In fact, value stocks are often the best stocks for various option-based strategies, assuming that you first apply the fundamental rules for stock selection.

Fundamentals of Stocks (with Options in Mind)

You need to determine the real meaning of "fundamental analysis" as part of an initial portfolio management technique. Without the fundamentals, how do you pick stocks? For investors who do not become familiar with an effective short list of indicators, selection of stocks is haphazard and inconsistent. This section presents the basic indicators every investor should master.

At the very least, you need five important indicators to establish fundamental criteria for selection of stocks. Beyond these five, a more serious analysis of accounting is necessary and, for most people, becomes more esoteric. The purpose in limiting this list to five indicators is to help you identify the beginning steps in picking stocks in companies that are well-managed, have a history of profits and dividend payments, and compete effectively in their sector. So before even reviewing the short list, begin your stock selection by identifying (1) sectors worth investing in, and (2) companies that dominate those sectors.

Sectors should be restricted to those producing better than average net profits. Most online brokerage services allow you to review basic indicators among companies within each sector as well as making sector-to-sector comparisons. A two-part elimination process will help you to narrow down your search to only those sectors in which companies are able to produce levels of profit attractive to you, and then to find the one or two companies that set the pace competitively. You will discover that a portfolio of strong, competitive, well-managed *value* companies also will be excellent stocks for many option strategies.

In any form of analysis, a single ratio or percentage outcome is not useful unless it is compared, either to another company or to the trend for the company itself. The long-term trend of a company's fundamentals reveals the story of what is going on. If a particular ratio, including any of the five basic tests, is erratic over time, you cannot depend on any future estimates. Thus, one of the attributes you should seek is a consistent and reliable trend in each of the fundamental tests.

Here are the five indicators to check for your list of potential investments.

INDICATOR 1. WORKING CAPITAL TEST—THE CURRENT RATIO

The first ratio (and trend) worth study is the test of working capital. The degree to which a company is able to manage its cash (including paying current bills in a timely manner) defines how well it is managed. If there is to be any prospect of dividend payments and future expansion, companies need to control working capital; the degree to which this is achieved is reported through the *current ratio*. This is a comparison between current assets and current liabilities.

A "current" asset or liability refers to a 12-month period. Assets in the form of cash or those convertible to cash within one year are classified as current. (These include cash, marketable securities, accounts and notes receivable, and inventory.) All liabilities payable within one year (including 12 months' payments on long-term liabilities) are classified as current. When current assets are divided by current liabilities, the result (expressed as a numerical value) is the current ratio. This formula is summarized in Figure 1-2.

EXAMPLE

If total current assets are $642,600 and current liabilities are $306,661, the current ratio is 2.1:

$642,600 ÷ $306,661 = 2.1

As a general standard, a current ratio of 2 or better is considered positive, but depending on the sector, current

FIGURE 1-2. CURRENT RATIO.

$$\frac{\text{current assets}}{\text{current liabilities}} = \text{current ratio}$$

ratios between 1 and 2 may also be positive. Whenever the current ratio is negative, it is a sign of poor working capital management.

You need to review the current ratio over a period of many years, looking for consistency. If a company maintains its current ratio, that establishes management's ability to plan ahead and to fulfill its obligations. Table 1-1, which presents a comparison between three companies in the same sector, reveals the importance of comparison over several years.

The table shows that for the oil and gas industry, current ratios below 2 are the norm. Exxon-Mobil is the strongest of the three companies, reporting steadily increasing working capital over a five-year period. BP has also been consistent, reporting a current ratio of 1 each year. And Royal Dutch Shell has improved over the period, but the first three years were below a current ratio of 1.

INDICATOR 2. CAPITALIZATION TEST—THE DEBT RATIO

Working capital is an essential feature in corporate financial management. It is a company's lifeline. Of equal importance is a company's capitalization structure. Total capitalization involves two parts. First is the equity, consisting of capital stock and retained earnings. Second is

TABLE 1-1. CURRENT RATIO COMPARISONS.

Fiscal year	Current ratio		
	Exxon-Mobil	BP	Royal Dutch Shell
2005	1.6	1.0	1.2
2004	1.4	1.0	1.1
2003	1.2	1.1	0.8
2002	1.2	1.0	0.8
2001	1.2	1.0	0.9

Source: Annual reports and S&P Stock Report summaries

long-term debt. A corporation funds its growth through a combination of equity and debt. But over time, it is important for a company to keep debt levels manageable. If debt rises over time, that means that in the future the company will have to pay ever-higher interest on that debt, as well as making repayments of the debt itself. So the higher the debt, the less profit is left to pay dividends or to finance expansion.

The *debt ratio* is the percentage of capitalization represented by debt. It is computed by dividing long-term debt by total capitalization, as shown in Figure 1-3.

EXAMPLE

Let's say a company's long-term debt is $1,009,646 and total capitalization (long-term debt plus total equity) is $3,536,046. The debt ratio in this case is 28.6 percent:

$1,009,646 ÷ $3,536,046 = 28.6%

In checking working capital, it is important also to check debt. By increasing the long-term debt level (making the debt ratio worse), a company can artificially create the appearance of strong working capital. For example, refer-

FIGURE 1-3. DEBT RATIO.

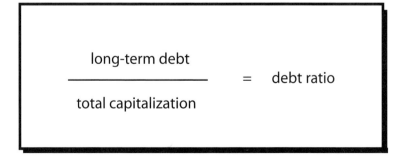

ring to the calculation of current ratio presented above, we stated that $642,600 ÷ $306,661 = 2.1. But what happens if the same company lost $450,000 in the following year, and current assets fell to $192,600? (Let's also assume that current liabilities remained about the same at $306,661.) That would create a *negative* current ratio, which would be very alarming. The company could simply issue a new bond worth $500,000. This improves the current ratio to $692,600 ÷ $306,661 = 2.3, an improvement over the past year. In this situation, the company reports an apparent improvement in the current ratio, even though it did so by committing itself to higher debt. In this case, equity capitalization would have remained about the same because the net loss was replaced by new debt. So the debt ratio would be:

$1,509,646 ÷ $3,536,046 = 42.7%

This demonstrates what happens when a company increases its long-term debt. The debt ratio rises, creating a weaker financial situation because of long-term interest obligations. Comparing a few well-known companies shows how good management and poor management affect the overall situation for a company. Table 1-2 summarizes a five-year debt ratio for four different companies.

This comparison demonstrates that companies are structured with vastly different capitalization models. It is not realistic to simply conclude that less debt is always an indication of a better-managed company. However, the trend is revealing. In the case of Johnson & Johnson, a very low debt ratio declined over the five-year period. Pfizer's did as well (with some fluctuations). Merck's increased slightly. Wyeth reported the highest debt ratio among the four, but it also declined.

The value in analyzing debt ratio is twofold. First, debt

TABLE 1-2. DEBT RATIO COMPARISONS.

Fiscal year	Johnson & Johnson	Pfizer	Merck	Wyeth
		Debt ratio		
2005	5.5	7.7	20.1	43.5
2004	7.4	8.3	19.2	44.2
2003	9.7	6.8	20.7	46.5
2002	8.0	13.4	17.4	48.1
2001	8.2	12.2	18.7	64.4

Source: Annual reports and S&P Stock Report summaries

ratio has to be studied along with the trend in the current ratio (especially in years when net losses are reported). Second, the trend is more revealing than the actual ratio level. When a company is able to reduce its long-term debt over several years, that is a positive sign. For example, in the case of General Motors, a rapidly declining profit picture was accompanied by a growing debt ratio over the same period:

Year	Net profit (in $ millions)	Debt Ratio
2005	$ – 10,458	91.0%
2004	2,805	85.5
2003	2,862	85.2
2002	1,736	89.0
2001	601	79.4

In this example, mounting annual net losses and ever-higher debt levels paint a dismal picture. The debt ratio trend—whether improving or deteriorating—is a very valuable indicator of a company's financial health.

INDICATOR 3. BASIC PROFITABILITY—NET EARNINGS

The third crucial test of a company's financial statements is basic profitability. It is amazing how many investors do

not check the profitability trend, considering how important it is in determining the stock's future value. A number
of specialized terms come into play when you check the
operating statement. These terms are summarized in Figure 1-4.

As you can see in the figure, the analysis moves from
the top to the bottom. Many people concentrate only on
the top (revenue) and the bottom (net earnings), but the
trends are crucial. Some important trend tests you can
apply should include:

- *Revenue growth.* Is the revenue line increasing over
  time, or decreasing? In the ideal situation, revenue
  should be growing each year.

- *Consistency of gross profit.* Growth in revenue is worthless if costs and expenses also increase. To tell whether
  the company is controlling its cost, the gross margin

FIGURE 1-4. SPECIALIZED TERMS IN CONSIDERING NET EARNINGS.

```
        Revenue
  -     Costs
        _____

  =     Gross Profit
  -     Expenses
        _____

  =     Operating Net Earnings
  +(-)  Other Income and Expenses
        _____

  =     Net Pretax Earnings
  -     Income Taxes
        _____

  =     Net Earnings
        ════════════
```

(gross profit divided by revenue) should remain the same year after year.

- *Consistency of expenses in relation to revenue.* The same argument applies to expenses. Too often, companies report higher revenues but expenses outpace that growth, resulting in lower net earnings. This occurs because expense controls are relaxed or managers reward themselves with higher pay.

- *Trend in operating net earnings.* The *operating net earnings* is one of the most important numbers on the operating statement because it reflects the trend in the primary business of the company: selling its product or services net of costs and expenses.

- *Comparison between net earnings and* core *net earnings.* The operating net earnings may include some nonrecurring items, so it gets distorted. For this reason, you should also track the so-called *core earnings* of the company. The concept was developed by Standard & Poor's to consistently track profits from the primary ("core") business of the company, excluding capital gains or losses, pro forma profits on invested pension assets, and other non-core types of profit, and to add in expenses not reported on the operating statement such as stock options rewarded to executives.

INDICATOR 4. CURRENT INCOME—THE DIVIDEND YIELD

The dividend yield is meaningful only based on the price you pay for stock. It is reported on a daily basis with ever-changing stock prices, but the yield you earn is always tied to the price you pay. The calculation involves dividing the annual dividend per share by the current price per share. This is shown in Figure 1-5.

The higher the stock's price moves, the lower the divi-

FIGURE 1-5. DIVIDEND YIELD.

$$\frac{\text{annual dividend per share}}{\text{current price per share}} = \text{dividend yield}$$

dend yield. It is a mathematically deceiving indicator for this reason. For example, if you purchase stock at $30 per share and the declared dividend is $1 per share, the yield you actually earn is 3.3 percent:

$1 \div \$30 = 3.3\%$

If the stock subsequently moves up to $32, then to $34 and to $36, the dividend yield falls:

$1 \div \$32 = 3.1\%$
$1 \div \$34 = 2.9\%$
$1 \div \$36 = 2.8\%$

But if the stock's price per share falls, dividend yield rises:

$1 \div \$28 = 3.6\%$
$1 \div \$26 = 3.8\%$
$1 \div \$24 = 4.2\%$

Because of these deceptive trends, you need to focus on the dividend per share based on the price you pay for shares of stock. Remember, though, that it is the trend that really counts. One effective way for picking high-value companies is to limit your search to companies that have consistently increased declared dividends over several years. The Mergent Company publishes very detailed stock reports for companies it calls "Dividend Achievers," defined as those companies that have increased dividends every year for at least ten years. Mergent's Dividend Achievers website is www.dividendachievers.com.

INDICATOR 5. STOCK VALUE—THE PRICE/EARNINGS RATIO

Some people think of a stock's "value" strictly in terms of its current price per share. However, this is misleading. A $20 stock could be more expensive than a $40 stock, for example, depending on the overall capital value of the company. Among the ways to tell a company's value is the P/E, the popular price/earnings ratio.

The P/E tells you how the market values the stock today. It is a calculation of an earnings multiple. The current price represents a value at a multiple of earnings, so that the higher the P/E, the more the stock is expected to grow in the future. To calculate this all-important ratio, the first step is to figure out a company's *earnings per share* (EPS). To calculate EPS, divide a full year's net earnings by the outstanding shares of common stock. The formula for EPS is shown in Figure 1-6.

Since the EPS is shown on free online brokerage research reports, you do not have to go through the calculation yourself. For example, the online site for Charles Schwab & Co. (https://investing.schwab.com) provides S&P Stock Reports to members, where the EPS and P/E ratio are provided. If you must calculate EPS by hand, apply the formula shown in Figure 1-6. The outstanding shares number might have changed for a company during the year, in which case you need to figure out the weighted average.

FIGURE 1-6. EARNINGS PER SHARE.

$$\frac{\text{total annual net earnings}}{\text{outstanding shares of common stock}} = \text{earnings per share}$$

The P/E ratio is calculated by dividing the current price per share by the EPS. The formula is summarized in Figure 1-7.

EXAMPLE

A company whose stock is selling today at $55 per share and with earnings per share of $3.85 has a P/E of 14:

$55 ÷ $3.85 = 14

The P/E in this example reveals that the market has priced the stock at a multiple of 14 times earnings. Most investors recognize that when P/E is exceptionally low (under 10, for example), there is little current interest in

FIGURE 1-7. PRICE/EARNINGS RATIO.

$$\frac{\text{current price per share}}{\text{latest reported earnings per share}} = \text{price/earnings ratio}$$

the stock and the price is likely to not show much growth. However, when P/E is high (above 30 or 35, for example), the stock's price will tend to be more volatile. So for most moderate investors, stocks with P/E between 12 and 25 are considered midrange.

In applying P/E as a test of whether or not to buy stock, or to narrow down a list of candidates, study the annual *range* of the P/E rather than the latest P/E by itself. Look for consistency over a long period of time. The research reports provided by online brokers are valuable for this purpose. The previously referenced S&P Stock Reports provide this to Charles Schwab account holders, for example. Table 1-3 compares three retail companies' low and high levels over a five-year period.

Note the disparity between the three retail stores. Although they are in the same industry, the companies' annual P/E ranges vary considerably. The earliest ratios for JC Penney (33 to 92) indicate a one-year price aberration in 2002, but all of these companies report their lowest P/E ranges during the same period. Most people will agree that any P/E over 25 is too high and likely to add to market risks, so this analysis is useful for making a comparison not only between companies but between years as well.

TABLE 1-3. PRICE/EARNINGS RATIO COMPARISONS.

| | P/E ratio | | | | | |
| | Federated | | J C Penney | | Kohl's | |
Year	low	high	low	high	low	high
2006	9	12	11	15	18	24
2005	11	15	11	19	19	26
2004	6	14	13	22	25	38
2003	7	14	11	22	24	42
2002	10	19	33	92	31	54

Source: Annual reports and S&P Stock Report summaries

A Technical Approach to Buying Stock

The fundamental approach is not the only way to pick stocks or options. Some people prefer the technical approach, a selection strategy based on a stock's price trends rather than on the financial trends reported by the company. Neither method is flawless, and in fact, both can be used together. If you plan to employ options as one way to manage portfolio risks and increase current income, many technical indicators can help you in timing your option trades.

The most important attribute revealed by a study of price movement is the level of price volatility. This translates to market risk. A stock with a broad trading range is less safe than one with a relatively narrow range. However, at the same time, stocks with very low volatility also offer less growth and less profit potential. You can combine fundamental and technical analysis to pick stocks that are suited to your risk profile and, at the same time, provide good opportunities in the option trades you will consider entering on that same stock.

A stock's trading range is simply the space between the high and low prices for the stock. This information is valuable when reviewed over a period of time. On a stock's chart, you can recognize the breadth and direction of the trading range over many months, which provides a visual summary of risk/opportunity. A trading range might maintain the same point spread, but it may be trending upward or downward. The range may also be broadening (showing a greater point range over time) or narrowing. These patterns are revealing to chartists, technicians who study stock price charts to time trades.

The boundaries of the trading range are also important. At the top is the *resistance level*, which is the highest price at which a stock has traded recently. At the bottom is the *support level*, the lowest price agreed upon by buyers and sellers. When price breaks through either resistance or support, it may signal the beginning of a significant price shift and act as the first step in establishing a new trading range at higher or lower price levels. When price moves close to either border of the trading range two or more times without breaking through, that price movement is believed to signal that the price is about to move in the opposite direction. So if price goes up to the resistance level without breaking through, that might signal an impending movement downward, even through and below the support level. The trading range, resistance level, and support level are summarized in Figure 1-8.

This figure displays various price patterns. Some are very predictable, and the longer a pattern holds, the more predictable the next entry becomes. By the same argument, when price is so volatile that no clear trading range, resistance level, or support level can be observed, it means that the volatility prevents any accurate estimates of future price movement.

Technical analysis also compares volatility of stocks. The traditional formula for defining a stock's volatility is to check price for the past year, and then divide the difference by the year's lowest price. This formula is summarized in Figure 1-9.

This calculation is flawed, however. Depending on the price range itself, the volatility is going to be distorted. Compare, for example, several different stocks whose annual trading range spanned 7 points:

$$(27 - 20) \div 20 = 35\%$$
$$(37 - 30) \div 30 = 23\%$$
$$(47 - 40) \div 40 = 17.5\%$$
$$(57 - 50) \div 50 = 14\%$$

FIGURE 1-8. TRADING RANGES.

level

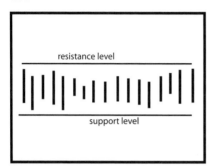

broadening

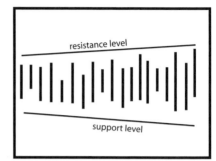

moving upward

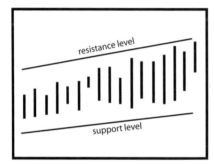

narrowing

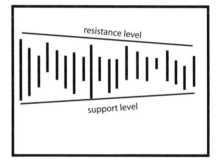

moving downward

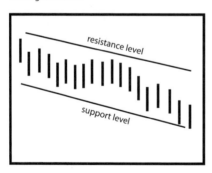

volatile

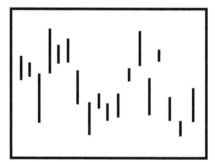

FIGURE 1-9. VOLATILITY.

$$\frac{\text{annual high} \; - \; \text{annual low}}{\text{annual low}} = \text{volatility}$$

In truth, all of these trading ranges were 7 points apart. Because the calculation depends on the existing and established trading range of the stock, this formula is not going to be accurate. If you define "volatility" as the point spread of a trading range, these distortions are misleading. Consider as well the effect of a price "spike." In statistics, accurate averaging calls for removal of spikes, as they distort the calculation. By definition, a spike is an aberrant price level that occurs and then does not recur. For example, if a stock has been trading between $40 and $47 per share, the traditional definition of volatility places it at 17.5%. But now consider what happens if, at any time during the year, the price of the stock jumps to $58 for two days, then returns to the range set below $47 and never returns to $58. Under the traditional calculation volatility is:

$(58 - 40) \div 40 = 45\%$

Realistically, the established trading range indicates that volatility is 17.5%. The inflexibility of the range test for volatility exaggerates the level. Another flaw in volatility is that it does not indicate current levels. For example, several different scenarios are possible, including:

- Prices were 7 points apart 52 weeks ago, but for the past 39 weeks, they have only been 3 points apart.

- Prices began at a very narrow 2 points, and they have been 7 points apart only during the last 52 weeks.

- The 7-point range has remained true while price levels have been rising.

- The 7-point range has remained true while price levels have been falling.

All of these possible variations of a 7-point trading range can and should be interpreted to mean different things in terms of risk, the trend itself, and the timing of purchase or sale of shares of stock. So for anyone using the traditional technical tests, it is crucial to be aware of the big picture and direction of price movement. In the selection of options for any portfolio strategy (creating income, taking profits, or insuring against price decline, for example), the true volatility *trend* is far more meaningful than the volatility percentage based on a 52-week trading range.

Understanding the Nature of Risk

A serious comparison of fundamental and technical indicators helps reduce your list of potential stocks. The comparison between companies as well as over time is instructive. In reviewing fundamental trends for ten years, it is glaringly easy to spot positive and negative trends.

For example, when revenues and net earnings rise consistently from year to year, or when current ratio and debt ratio remain constant, it is clear that a company's management is keeping things in mind, both in terms of operating profits and working capital. On the technical side, consistently low volatility is an encouraging sign of correspondingly low risk. Companies whose profits improve over time invariably also experience rising stock prices. All of this has great relevance in the options market.

Higher-risk companies (whose fundamentals change rather than improve gradually) tend to have options with greater short-term value. This is true because of the uncertainty in the immediate future. Greater market risk of stocks translates to the same level of risk in options. This also presents potentially greater profits from well-selected option strategies. The relationship between risk and potential is inseparable. For those who restrict their portfolio to only stocks, the volatility risk is a troubling one, and is thus a big problem. But if you combine a long-term stock investment strategy with an options strategy, the risk can be managed to create profits and avoid losses. This is the key to using options as part of your overall approach to stock market investing. Options are often touted as a means for fast riches, but that exaggeration misses the point. Options are far better used to enhance current income, take stock profits in short-term price swings, and protect against downside price risk.

The usual presentation of stock analysis involves the mechanics of the numbers, so you will discover how to divide one value into another to create a ratio, and then decide whether the outcome is good or bad. One aspect of a more evolved strategy may involve the use of such analysis to continually check and recheck the value of a corporation. (As defined by value investors, "value" stock is selling below intrinsic value, in companies that are exceptionally competitive and well-managed.) So on the one hand, analysis can and should be used to ensure that your portfolio contains value stocks with great potential for long-term appreciation; on the other hand, the stocks in your portfolio can be managed, protected, and maximized with options.

This brings up one of the most important aspects of

stock market (and option) risks. There is a tendency to review risk as an isolated attribute of each company or of the stock market, and to consider option risk as an entirely separate type of risk. But in fact, stock and option risks are directly related and should be analyzed as part of the same trend. Of course, stocks demonstrating higher volatility also are associated with higher than average option premium levels. These are two aspects of the same risk. From the risk perspective, the "perfect" company for your portfolio should offer a combination of risk-related attributes, including:

- *Moderate levels of volatility.* This is important because risk and growth potential are related. Thus, a very narrow and unchanging trading range is not going to offer as great a profit potential as a more volatile stock.

- *True measures of value.* Some investors confuse a stock's price with the concept of value. Thus, they see a lower-priced stock as a better value. Of course, the real definition of value means the stock is available at a bargain price. A related and equally important test involves competition and management, which are issues that are not specifically measurable as financial trends. A worthwhile value investment should be highly competitive within its sector and also be extremely well-managed.

- *Better than average dividend yield.* As a general observation, companies paying higher than average dividends are most likely to also manage their working capital. If you seek companies whose dividends have been increased every year for the past ten years, you are also more likely to find exceptionally strong long-term investments.

Applying these criteria in stock selection, you are also likely to find a robust volume of trading in options. The first test should always be to fill your portfolio with a few stocks of superior quality, purchased at a reasonable or bargain price, whose companies are exceptionally well managed and clearly competitively dominant. If you apply these criteria in stock selection, you are likely to identify a small number of stocks that are suitable. Owning three to five exceptional stocks is a better approach than owning 10 to 20 stocks in companies of average or mediocre value.

■ The Basic Option Rules of the Game

In the larger context of identifying appropriate risks and finding stocks, any use of options should be undertaken with the basic "rules" in mind. These rules follow.

Basic Option Rule 1. The Option Strategies You Use Have to Be a Good Match for Your Risk Tolerance. No matter how logically you can come up with reasons to use options, they must be an appropriate match for your level of risk. Remember, options can be very high-risk or very low-risk. One mistake investors make is chasing option profits in a way that exceeds their risk tolerance or places their long-term portfolio in jeopardy. There is a wide range of possible strategies you can employ; your first rule should be that they fit within your investing goals and risk tolerance level.

A lot of market insiders talk about risk tolerance without really understanding what it means. For many, the term implies that some investors are conservative and careful, whereas others are more speculative in how they invest. While this comparison is true, it does not define the full scope of "risk tolerance." The attributes of this concept (which are expanded in Chapter 2) have to include experience and knowledge, personal bias for or against particular industries or companies, the amount of investment capital available to you, your annual income and personal budget, and living status (married or single, rent or own, number of children, etc.). All of the aspects of your life define you as an investor and, as a result, establish your true risk tolerance. It is not just the degree of recklessness you are willing to take (the usual definition of risk tolerance) but how much risk you understand and can afford.

Basic Option Rule 2. You Need to Completely Understand the Risk of Any Strategy You Use. The second big mistake investors make is entering an option position without appreciating the real risks they face. For this reason, you do need to develop a working knowledge of options, perhaps using one of the many paper trading sites to try out strategies before you put real money into a position. (Basically, paper trading is a dry run of a strategy.) The Chicago Board Options Exchange (CBOE) offers listings, tutorials, and paper trading for options at its website (www.cboe.com). Many other sites provide you with free paper trading capabilities. A search for *"option paper trading" + free* will produce many results worth checking out and is an excellent method for seeing how real-time option trading works.

Paper trading is a great method for learning about options without losing money. Not only will you discover flaws in your assumptions, but you will also learn the specific language of options along the way. Even experienced traders have to struggle to understand how and why option values change as they do. If options were merely responsive to movement of a stock's price, it would be easy to profit from trading options. But these instruments are more complex, and their values change for reasons not always specifically related to stock movement. Only with paper trading can you learn the market without *expensive* experience.

Basic Option Rule 3. Your First Goal Should Be to Maximize and Protect Your Stock Positions. Any option-based profits are secondary. Your stock portfolio is and should be your first priority. Among the many ways that options can be traded, outright speculation is the most popular. But about 75 percent of all options expire worthless, so this is a difficult area to make a profit consistently. The real value in options is found in those strategies aimed at making your stock portfolio safer and more profitable.

Many more investors would be likely to include options as portfolio management tools if the presentation of the market were balanced. All too often, the approach offered by stockbrokers, analysts, and other insiders involves one of two concepts. First is the idea that you can "play" in the market with options, perhaps making a lot of money in a matter of only a few hours. (Often not mentioned is the equal opportunity to lose money in the same short time span.) Second is a complete separation of option strategies from stock portfolio strategies. As a consequence, conservative "value" investors, who like long-term, carefully selected stocks, tend to ignore options altogether. And that could be a mistake. Even the most conservative investor can be true to the well-understood goals of the long-term portfolio while using options.

Basic Option Rule 4. All Option Strategies Should Be Entered with a Clear Exit Strategy. To succeed in the options market, you also have to follow your own rules. It is ironic that many option traders forget to define how or when they will exit the position. Without an exit strategy, you program an options strategy to fail.

Consider the likely range of outcomes: If the option's

value increases, you will want to continue holding onto it in the hope that it will rise even farther. If the option's position declines, you will want to keep it until the price rebounds. But when do you close the position? The solution to this dilemma is to identify a clear exit point. For example, given that option values can and do change dramatically, you could set a goal for yourself to exit a position when you either double your investment or lose one-half of its original value.

Basic Option Rule 5. Realize that the Market Rewards Patience. This is especially true when you combine stock and option positions in the same portfolio. Patient traders often create more profits than impatient ones. Some traders are attracted to the option market because they enjoy the fast action. But if you sell only when you have small profits, and continue holding on to depreciated options (and stocks), you will end up with a portfolio of depreciated assets. You will see a better long-term outcome if you buy and hold stocks for the long term and wait out the right opportunities to use options.

The time element itself is what makes options so perfect for the patient investor. Some strategies are highly conservative and profitable and actually benefit from time. In the popular option strategies involving buying contracts and hoping for price increases as quickly as possible, time is the enemy. But it does not have to be. The fact that 75 percent of all options expire worthless points the way to option profits, even in the most conservative long-term portfolio.

Basic Option Rule 6. Be Aware of All Possible Outcomes. The best option strategy is one you enter in which you are prepared to accept any of those outcomes. Any time an investor is surprised by the outcome of a strategy, it usually means money was lost instead of gained. Wise option trading involves worst-case analysis in addition to an appreciation for profit potential. The best strategy is one in which the worst-case outcome will be profitable. You cannot fail if you will be pleased with any of the possible outcomes. (These generally include exercise, expiration, or closing the position.) Which outcome is ideal? The best possible trade is an option trade that produces profits in *all* of these possible outcomes. In coming chapters, many such strategies are compared and explained.

If you meet active option traders, you hear a lot of "what if" discussion. If only you had bought a particular option at a different time, or sold when it was higher, or picked a different stock . . . the character of the market defines the kinds of traders and speculators who are so often found actively trading options.

The wise use of options not as a stand-alone speculative device but as a tool within your long-term portfolio is going to be profitable and sensible. The purpose should not be primarily to speculate but to protect portfolio positions and enhance current income. Chapter 2 begins by offering some ideas for setting portfolio goals and defining acceptable risks.

SETTING PORTFOLIO
AND RISK GOALS

"If you do not think about the future, you cannot have one."
—John Galsworthy, *Swan Song*, 1928

I T IS ALL TOO EASY for long-term plans to go off course. When your portfolio is designed as a good match for your goals (in terms of risk, for example), you are on the right track. But for many investors, over time the portfolio changes, and so do the goals. When a portfolio ends up being a poor match for your goals, you are in trouble.

In this chapter, essential portfolio planning attributes are presented and explained in terms of how you might use options. However, as with any plan, even a sound option strategy for one person is not appropriate for another. When the conditions of your life change, your portfolio has to keep up. The major occurrences in life that may radically change your investing goals include marriage, change of career, buying a home, having children, divorce, and illness. Any of these events can certainly threaten your investment portfolio's overall health, not to mention the risks you face and the types of products you need to select.

Since you have to balance multiple concerns in your portfolio, it is important to define what you want to achieve. You have to be concerned with market risk and liquidity and with the fortunes of a company that might be strong today but not necessarily in the future.

EXAMPLE

If you look back 50 or 75 years, some of the strongest and most dominant companies in the United States were General Motors, Kodak, and ITT. Today, the situation has changed dramatically. The market is now dominated by foreign cars, digital cameras, and numerous telephone companies (including cellular technology), all of which were difficult to imagine only a few decades ago. It is also likely that in the future, the same kinds of technological advances will make many of today's strongest industries obsolete. The difficulty is in knowing which ones will suffer from future changes.

No portfolio can be set in stone as a permanent and safe collection of stocks. In the past, this was precisely what many insiders suggested—and, in fact, the mutual fund industry grew largely on that premise. Today's portfolio is more likely to change rapidly as various sectors come into favor or fall out of favor. Examining various kinds of risk reveals exactly how you can build your portfolio with your goals in mind and how options can help to keep those risks under control.

The Real Meaning of Market Risk

Market risk is the endless concern of investors. For some, it is an obsession. The daily stock price movements dominate the time for many, including those who describe themselves as "long-term investors" or "value investors." All of the fundamental theories tell you that short-term price changes do not matter, yet the majority of people with money at risk follow prices not only by the day but often by the hour.

This all-important risk affects how people invest, as it should. But risk does not have to be an fixation. Instead, you can have the best of both worlds: You can pick moderately volatile stocks with excellent prospects for long-term growth *and* take advantage of the market's tendency to overreact to virtually everything. The key to this approach is the selective use of options. The more troubling market risk is to you, the more likely you are to find options an excellent method for cushioning that risk, and even turning it into potential profit rather than exposure to loss.

The financial media make this information available virtually everywhere. You can create your own stock ticker on your XM Radio; get endless information on many financial news television stations; and, of course, find streaming quotes for your portfolio on your computer, at home as well as at work. For anyone who enjoys being a "stock ticker junkie," there are plenty of dealers out there. Market risk is continually kept in front of everyone, and you are constantly reminded (especially while the markets are open) that the slightest blips in consumer confidence, oil prices, interest rates, earnings, or new products are likely to cause *your* stock's price to soar or to plummet.

What does market risk really mean? Is it limited to the endless plus and minus price movements? Some stocks are quite erratic and tend to move with the market, often in exaggerated fashion. But with a long-term perspective, even volatile stocks are going to change in price over many months or years based on the company's fundamentals. Some market watchers like to argue that technical and fundamental analysis cannot be reconciled. One is focused on price and volume, the other on earnings and working capital. In fact, though, the two are different aspects of the same concept. Some basics of investing in corporations are worth keeping in mind when analyzing market risk. A discussion of these basics follows.

WELL-MANAGED, COMPETITIVE COMPANIES GROW IN VALUE OVER TIME

While this might be obvious to most people, it is a profound observation—if only because investors sometimes act as though it were not true. In picking stocks, a widespread tendency is to make decisions based on rumor, popularity, and market sentiment, often without even considering the real value of the company or whether the stock is a sound bargain at its current price. One reason that so many investors pick the wrong stocks is that they forget to look at the basics. It is like buying a new car based on its color rather than on its price, mileage, or extras.

What does "well-managed" mean? You can define excellence in management in a number of ways, including a review of the numbers. For example, how much compensation does the top management take? Is the compensation justified by performance? When you review growth in revenues, are net profits keeping pace? It is not a positive sign if revenues are growing but profits are shrinking; in fact, it is shameful that management allows such a trend to occur at all, and it is the stockholders who end up suffering the consequences of poor (or self-serving) management policies.

A "competitive" company is easy to spot. If you have decided to own stock in a particular sector, you can define that sector's leader by its financial strength, revenue levels and growth, earnings, and other financial outcomes—

especially in a long-term trend. The leader tends to out-grow its competitors and to control and dominate a large share of the market.

FINANCIAL TRENDS DIRECTLY AFFECT STOCK PRICES

Many investors don't recognize the relationship between financial strength and price growth (or a weakening financial position and price decline). The relationship is easily observed over time, as a comparison between companies demonstrates. Figure 2-1 shows the nine-year history of price range and net income for Wal-Mart. The scale to the left is for annual high and low price levels, and the scale on the right is for net income reported per year. Note that both price range and net income increased at Wal-Mart.

FIGURE 2-1. PRICE RANGE AND NET INCOME FOR WAL-MART.

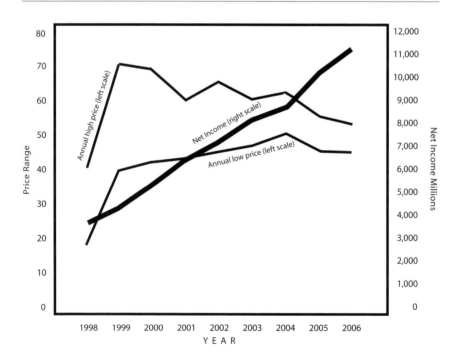

A similar analysis for General Motors, shown in Figure 2-2, makes the point that financial strength or weakness is related directly to price trends. In the case of GM, both price range and net income move in the opposite direction.

SHORT-TERM VOLATILITY (MARKET RISK) IS AN ATTRIBUTE OF PROFIT POTENTIAL IN THE LONG TERM

You are likely to find price volatility disturbing. What does it mean if a stock's price gyrates wildly in reaction to overall market trends, internal news, or trends within its own

FIGURE 2-2. PRICE RANGE AND NET INCOME FOR GENERAL MOTORS.

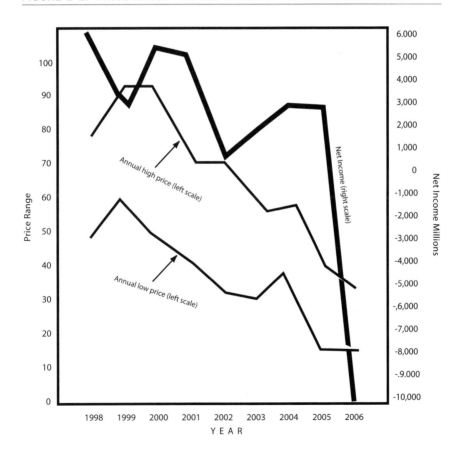

sector? Is volatility and short-term market risk always indicative of long-term market risk?

One effective method for picking stocks is to make decisions based on both financial trends and price volatility. Market risk, most often observed in price volatility, also represents an opportunity for price appreciation. For example, if the fundamentals are quite strong but price volatility is high, you have an opportunity. Waiting for the price to trend low creates a bargain. Under the rules of value investing, you want to buy shares of companies with strong fundamentals, but at a bargain price.

The second aspect of this approach is to use options to take advantage of short-term price volatility. Thus, after you buy shares of such a company at a bargain price, you can exploit the market's emotional overreaction in both price directions to create profits—while keeping shares as long-term investments. For most people, this solves one of the biggest problems in the market. Do you take profits when prices rise? Do you sell when prices fall to cut losses? As long as the company continues to be a valid long-term hold, you can exploit those short-term price movements without selling shares. This is one of the most effective uses of options.

THERE IS A DANGER OF BECOMING OVERLY CONCERNED WITH SHORT-TERM PRICE CHANGES AND WITH ASSIGNING SHORT-TERM TRENDS TOO MUCH WEIGHT

Even investors who describe themselves as "conservative" or "long-term" are susceptible to short-term temptation. Remember, as long as the stock you select remains a positive investment as defined by value investment principles, those short-term price movements are not important. Some of the wiser value investors even advise that people should pick stocks wisely and then turn off their TV, stop reading newspapers, and stop checking their stocks online four times a day.

This advice makes sense if you are going to worry constantly about profit and loss in the short term. Keep focused on the idea that well-selected value companies are going to reward you in the long term. But let's also take value investing a step further. You should ignore price movements in the sense of trying to decide whether you should sell your shares; as long as the company remains well-managed, competitive, and fairly priced, you want to keep those shares. At the same time, however, you can observe minor point changes on a daily basis and use options as a type of secondary plan on those shares: protecting profits when prices might fall, taking profits when prices are high, and insuring your portfolio if and when the market does fall in triple digits.

An enlightened definition of market risk accounts primarily for long-term growth opportunities and not for daily price movement. Value companies do experience price growth along with ever-improving revenues and earnings, so those companies are the very ones you want to have in your portfolio. Thus, there are two important aspects concerning market risk. First, in the short term it does not matter what price changes occur, because your focus is on the broader time horizon. Second, short-term volatility defined as "market risk" can be exploited through options to maximize current income, so the risk itself is the reverse side of the opportunity coin.

If you focus on day-to-day (or hour-to-hour) price changes, then you are acting more like a speculator than a long-term investor. This trap is common, and many moderate and conservative investors, while continuing to believe in value-based principles, end up reacting to short-term market trends. This is a big mistake. The solution, however, is not to become more disciplined or more focused on the distant future. The solution is to work with the advantages of value investing *and* option trading. You can maintain a well-selected portfolio of value stocks while using options to play the short-term price trends and to turn market risk into market profit.

Knowledge Risk

Knowledge is essential in the case of the options market. Everyone who owns stock needs to develop his or her knowledge base, so that research, sector selection, and timing are all based on a sensible analytical program. This involves a balance between experience and research, because no one has the time to look at every company or to apply every possible formula to evaluate companies. When it comes to risk, it is accurate to say that anyone considering using options faces a *lack* of knowledge risk.

The options market is complex in terms of its jargon and special rules and how prices change. For this reason, the well-earned reputation that options are high-risk and exotic is often valid. However, you can limit your risk if you select a few specific strategies and know when and how to use them—but you need the knowledge to make these decisions. Gaining knowledge takes effort, and *knowledge risk* is the risk that you will make decisions within your portfolio without understanding the possible outcomes.

There are a few levels of knowledge risk worth knowing about, each of which can be overcome through analysis and study. The market is never so complex that you cannot master the obstacles. Gaining knowledge provides you with the means for effectively creating profits through options. These levels of knowledge risk include:

• *Options terminology.* For most first-time option traders, terminology is daunting. More than any other factor, the specialized terminology creates the impression of high risk and gives options an even greater exotic flavor than they actually have. Insiders easily overlook the intimidating factor for newcomers and, in some cases, may even think of the highly specialized terminology as a way to "keep out the riffraff." In other words, some insiders like to think of the options market as a private club. With the easy and affordable accessibility of the Internet, however, options are becoming less exclusive and more practicable for a growing population of investors—in spite of the complexities of terminology and insider jargon.

• *Trading rules and restrictions.* Every potential option trader needs to understand the basic rules and restrictions of the industry. The disclosure brochure *Characteristics and Risks of Standardized Options* explains all of the essential rules, risks, and preliminary terms you need to know. This document is important reading, and it can be downloaded free from the Options Clearing Corporation (OCC) at www.optionsclearing.com/publications/risks/riskstoc.pdf.

Among the important rules are those explaining how and when options can be exercised on both long and short position sides, types of strategies, and margin requirements. Beyond this booklet, you also need to be aware of special rules for high-level trading (see Chapter 4) and the specific margin requirements for each type of option strategy. In addition, each broker provides trading levels for each account in which options are traded, restricting the kinds of transactions you are allowed to execute; this is determined by your experience in option trading and also by the cash value of your portfolio and cash accounts.

• *Stock price movement and consequences for option position.* Even the most experienced option trader has to remain alert. Movement of a stock's price affects option premium levels. At times, however, the option premium overreacts or underreacts to the changes in price; this enigmatic aspect of option trading is both interesting and frustrating. There are no automatic triggers affecting option values. Of course, you expect a specific kind of reaction, so that price movement should occur in the same direction as stock. But this is most true when the option's strike price is closest to the current stock price *and* when expiration is close. When large price gaps are found between the strike price and current stock value—and when expiration is a long way off—price movement is less clear. In fact, options can reveal a perplexing lack of response even to strong stock price movement based on time remaining until expiration.

With experience, you will begin to recognize the interaction between price, time, and proximity (of stock price to option strike price), and how the reliance of these three specific elements are related to the nonspecific market attributes. Those include market interest in the stock (reflected in the P/E ratio, for example), the stock's trading range and price volatility, trading volume in the stock (and in various options on that stock), and corporate news (earnings reports and forecasts, acquisitions or spinoffs, changes in management, and new product announcements).

Investment Goals

Most people have heard all about goal setting as an important step in the development of a budget, a financial plan, or a new business. But goals are only as good as the context they are given. For example, your goals in investing might include the usual (saving to buy a house, retire, or put children through college); how you reach those goals depends not on specific investments but on the strategies you employ along the way.

In the usual financial planning literature, you are told to dollar cost average, reinvest dividends, and define criteria for picking stocks. Looking beyond these rather obvious tactical approaches to investing, it makes more sense to overlay your long-term personal goals with strategic investing goals. These are related to how income is generated, reinvested, and managed; how much risk is appropriate in your portfolio; and how you divide up your capital among various investment programs.

This allocation of assets is often too easily geared toward a formula. You can go online, for example, and find websites that will tell you to allocate your total portfolio 25 percent in real estate, 55 percent in stocks, and 20 percent in cash. But why? How can a broad, blanket recommendation like that be made without first examining your personal risk tolerance, age, income, experience, and life situation? The answer, of course, is that allocation has to be based on the specific goals and other attributes, and that within a portfolio of stocks, you can employ some very specific strategies to maximize investment return.

A basic strategy, for example, is to reinvest all of your stock dividends. Through dividend reinvestment, you create compound returns on current income. On most brokerage sites, you can specify at the time you buy shares that you want automatic dividend reinvestment. If your broker does not provide this capability, you can enter into your own Dividend Reinvestment Plan (DRIP) by purchasing directly. Check the site www.wall-street.com for an example of how this can be done.

Dividend income can play a significant role in your portfolio, especially over the long term. Through reinvestment, you not only get a compound return on the dividend; you also increase your basis in shares of stock, so that potential capital gains will be greater in the future as well.

To augment your portfolio, you first set goals based on why you invest. But that is just a starting point with the purpose of deciding how much risk is appropriate. In spite of what traditional financial planning concepts tell you, goal setting does not lead you to a specific investment. It only sets borders on the kinds of risks you can and should take. Once you know the appropriate kind of risk, you can next determine the range of investments you want to pursue. The context of defining risks suited to your goals is perhaps the best way to know what kind of return you need from your portfolio of stocks.

This leads you to a dilemma: What if your risk profile limits you to a range of stocks that might not yield enough return to meet your goals? Most people have to face this reality at some point and decide on a course of action, including:

- Taking greater risks, hopefully to increase portfolio yields

- Changing goals to lower expectations

- Planning to continue working longer than originally planned

- Reducing living expenses (for example, accelerating your 30-year mortgage payment to a level that will pay it off in 20 years)

- Taking a second job

All of these measures involve serious changes, either in risk profile or quality of life. However, another way to close the gap between expectations and likely yield is with the use of options. This does not mean taking higher risks, because the kinds of option strategies you choose have to be a sound match for your risk profile. Fortunately, this is possible. Even very conservative investors can employ low-risk option strategies to increase current income. (The precise strategies for this are explained in Chapter 4.) As far as the discussion of investment goals is concerned, the key point to remember is this: You do not need to alter your expectations or take higher risks to increase your portfolio yield.

How Options Help with Your Investment Goals

To provide a quick overview of how options work to help you realize your income goals without increasing risks, here is range of strategies to consider. (These will be explained in detail in later chapters.)

COVERED CALLS

The best conservative strategy is the covered call. This involves owning 100 shares of stock and writing (selling) a call. By doing this, you grant the right to a buyer to call away your 100 shares at the fixed strike price. So if the stock's value rises above that price, you will be required to sell your stock below market value. As long as the strike price is higher than your purchase price, this results in a profit, in three ways. First, you earn a capital gain when the stock is called away. Second, when you sell a call you receive the premium, which you keep. Third, as long as you own the stock, you are entitled to dividends.

Some people point out that when you sell a call, you might give up future price appreciation, and that is true. However, remember that 75 percent of all options expire worthless, so while this does happen it usually does not. Later, you will see how you can avoid exercise when stock values do rise, so you can either keep your stock or accept exercise at an even higher strike price. Covered call writing is a very conservative strategy when done properly. It is entirely likely that you can create double-digit return on your investment every year with covered calls without increasing your market risk.

Using Options for Profit Taking and Bargain Hunting

The stockholder's dilemma is that short-term prices move around. If you want to hold stock for the long term, it makes no sense to sell whenever prices rise, and it also makes no sense to panic and sell when prices fall. With options, you can take advantage of short-term price movement without touching your long-term portfolio. When a stock's price rises several points, you can write a covered call or buy a long put. In both cases, you expect the price to reverse and retreat in the opposite direction. If that happens, the covered call loses value and you can purchase to close at a profit. Or, the long put will also increase in value as the stock price falls, so it can be sold at a profit. Both of these strategies enable you to take profits without selling stock, and without high risk.

When a stock's price falls, you can take advantage of the short-term decline without selling stock. When prices fall quickly, you can buy long calls on the theory that the price is likely to turn around and move back up. A higher-risk strategy is to sell uncovered puts. While these are not as risky as selling uncovered calls, they do involve a degree of risk. However, if your timing is right and the stock's price rises, the short put will decline in value and it can be closed (bought) at a profit.

USING LONG PUTS FOR INSURANCE

If you have observed that your stock's price has risen significantly, it is natural to be concerned. Other stockholders might want to take profits, which could cause the stock's price to retreat. To protect paper profits, you can buy puts as a form of portfolio insurance. Under this plan, if the stock's price does fall, you can sell the put and take a profit. In this way, the decline in your stock's value is offset by the profit in your long put.

SHORT PUTS AS A FORM OF CONTINGENT STOCK PURCHASE

A more advanced strategy is to sell uncovered puts with a plan to eventually allow exercise, as a means of buying stock. This is an advanced strategy, however, and not appropriate for the novice. If the put is exercised, you will be buying stock at a price above current market value. The difference between the strike price and market value, less the premium you receive for selling the put, represents the paper loss. However, if you consider the strike price a reasonable price for stock, selling a put is one way to create current income.

If you do end up having stock put to you at a price above current market value, you can adjust the loss in two ways. First, the put premium you received is yours to keep. Second, once you own the stock, you can sell a covered call to make up the paper loss. As with all option strategies, you need to check the numbers for a variety of possible outcomes and make sure that the strategy makes sense.

ADVANCED STRATEGIES

There are a limitless number of possible advanced strategies, appropriate only for experienced option traders *and* only when you fully understand the risk levels. One effective strategy creates current income with minimal risk. It involves two stages. First, you write a covered call on 100 shares of stock you own. Second, you sell a put. The income you get from selling both the call and the put is yours to keep; it also reduces the potential difference between the strike price and current market value of stock if and when the put is exercised. This strategy, called contingent purchase, is explained in detail in Chapter 6.

Using a combination of covered call and uncovered put makes sense as long as you are willing to assume the risk of buying more shares; the premium levels justify that risk; and you are comfortable with all possible outcomes. As long as you accept these conditions, the advanced contingent purchase strategy is actually a conservative one and can create double-digit returns on stock in many cases.

How and Why Investment Goals Change

Using numerous strategies, options can be used to increase current income, reduce risks, and enable you to keep your portfolio intact. These strategies cover the gamut from extremely high-risk to extremely conservative, and this is where your opportunity lies. At the same time, it is wise to recognize that investment goals change, and when they do, your risk profile changes as well. That usually means you need to shift to a different range of investment strategies, including both stocks and options.

Goals change because of major life events. If those changes also alter your actual risk profile, then last year's strategies are not going to be appropriate any longer. Just as goals and risks change, so must the stocks you select to include in your portfolio, as well as your portfolio management attributes. For example, your use of options may need to shift from one risk profile to another.

EXAMPLE

You consider your risk tolerance fairly high, so you have been taking some chances. These have included investing in volatile stocks, writing uncovered puts, and writing partially covered calls (called a "ratio write," this involves writing more calls than stock, such as writing four calls against 300 shares). None of these strategies are at the extreme end of the spectrum, but they contain more risk than most people want. Now things have suddenly changed. During the past year, you and your spouse bought a house and had a child. You find that more of your budget has to go toward life, disability, homeowners, and health insurance than before. You know you cannot afford the level of risk you accepted in the past.

In the situation described in the above example, the entire "life circumstances" changed. It would be appropriate to review the whole portfolio, get rid of exceptionally volatile stocks, and replace them with strong blue chips, high-yielding dividend stocks, and good growth stocks. Rather than tempting fate with short options, you might also consider limiting your option trades to covered calls, puts for insurance after price growth, and occasional long positions to take advantage of strong price movement. In other words, the changed circumstances in your life demand a review not only of what is in your portfolio but also of what risks work with your new risk profile.

It is amazing how profoundly these changes affect risk profile. The important events like marriage, buying a house, having a child, or changing careers often require a complete rethinking of your entire approach to investing. On the negative side, events like divorce, a serious illness or death in the family, or loss of a job also have undeniable impact on how and where you invest. Sadly, few people make the required changes they need to adjust risk profile *and* to ensure that their portfolio strategies are a good match.

It is reasonable to suggest than an annual review of your portfolio, your risk tolerance, your long-term goals, and your specific strategies is a minimal requirement. You do not need to hire a financial planner to tell you when things have changed; you already know how your life and financial health has evolved in recent months. You need to undergo the review on a regular basis, especially immediately after important changes have taken place. You know that the kinds of risks appropriate for a single person age 25 are rarely the same as those for a 35-year-old married homeowner with children. That is obvious, but it only helps to acknowledge the changes if you act by making changes in your portfolio to reflect a changed risk tolerance, and only if you also adjust the strategies you employ.

Many people call themselves "fundamental" investors, but they act like technical investors, moving money in and out of stocks and options based on partial-point movement, daily financial news or rumor, or advice from their barber, co-worker, or best friend. That problem—thinking you are of one profile but acting under another—just scratches the surface of the risk profile problem. Of course, all investors need to make sure that the basis for their decisions is in line with their risk profile. (This, again, is an obvious piece of advice, but one rarely followed.) When major goals also change, the portfolio and its strategies need a complete makeover as well.

Risk and Changing Markets

In coordinating a stock portfolio with the strategic use of options, one eye should remain on ever-evolving personal goals, risk tolerance, and appropriate investments. At the same time, your selection of specific stocks or options is going to be affected by the markets as well. The idea of "market risk" is, to put it in the most obvious form, the risk that stock values will fall when you have expected them to rise.

Markets change and, if you follow the long-term broad market view, you know that bull markets and bear markets can last several months or even years. When the economy goes through a recession, it usually means several weak signs at once: rising unemployment and interest rates, falling or weak stock prices, a level or falling housing market, and rising inflation. When market direction changes, so must investment strategies. If you limit your portfolio to only stocks, you often have to just hold on through tough times, hoping a recession will not last too long. But one of the great attributes of options is that they can produce profits in many different kinds of markets. Depending on the direction the market is moving, an option strategy can be found that will produce profits.

These points refer to long-term market trends, which technicians call *primary* trends. Don't confuse these with momentary price adjustments, which tend to be limited to one, two, or three days and which also tend to reverse completely within weeks. For example, at the end of February 2007, the market—as measured by the Dow Jones Industrial Average (DJIA)—fell more than 400 points in one day. The following day, another smaller decline occurred. Some people were concerned that this was the beginning of a sudden and complete reversal in the market. But cooler heads doubted this, aware that so many economic signals were positive. Unemployment, interest rates, and inflation were at record-low levels, while other economic signs continued to show positive direction. Within three weeks, the market was nearly back where it had started. The DJIA was not at its previous high level, but most stocks had come back strongly after the two-day decline.

These types of short-term spikes in averages are not uncommon. There is never a shortage of people who are going to worry about any big change and who fail to recognize that the markets tend to be volatile. But when a decline stops after two days and the averages then emerge as strongly as they were before, that is a sign that the decline merely reflected a temporary overreaction. The markets in Asia had fallen the day before the U.S. markets fell, with the same reaction in the European stock markets. The U.S. markets were simply following that trend, but the U.S. economy was strong enough to recover rapidly.

The lesson to be learned from this is that the stock market is going to rise and fall in the short term, and bull or bear trends are cyclical. However, when a primary trend is firmly established and the overall direction of the market changes, that also signals the need for a change in portfolio strategies. The stocks you own today might not do well if and when the market's direction changes. However, regardless of the trend, if you have picked good value stocks, they will remain sound long-term investments even if the market becomes very weak.

At such times, you can effectively use options to exploit a downward movement in the averages. Even sound long-term companies are likely to go through a period of price weakness. Traditionally, if you wanted to keep the stock, you had to go through the decline and hope prices would rebound. But with options, you can use a downward trend to generate *higher* short-term income. In coming chapters, you will find many of these defensive moves, in which options can both protect your portfolio positions and create new sources of income.

Before proceeding into the actual strategic range of options, you are going to need to master the terminology of this market. Chapter 3 sets up your journey into the world of options by explaining what all of the jargon really means.

THE STRANGE WORLD
OF OPTIONS LINGO

"Nowadays to be intelligible is to be found out."
—Oscar Wilde, *Lady Windermere's Fan*, 1892

ONE INHIBITING FACTOR about the options market is its language. The exotic and highly specialized terminology used by option traders often creates the impression that this market is too high-level and advanced for the average investor. The truth, however, is that by mastering a few terms and learning to apply them to specific situations, you can overcome the "language barrier" and develop proficiency in this high-potential market.

The best way to learn any language is to situate yourself in an environment where that language is spoken. For the novice, an online search for *"option trading"* + *"chat room"* will lead to several sites where other traders talk the lingo. A word of caution, however: It is not advisable to make trades based on anything you see in a chat room, because you have no idea who the other people are or what their incentive is for giving advice. Stock "tips" and option plays should not serve as a basis for buying, just as a method for learning the language of options.

The Basic Language

The handful of important terms you need to learn relates to the mechanics of how options are distinguished from one another, valued, and traded. There are potentially hundreds of terms you will encounter with any type of trading; the dictionary link at the online resource Investopedia (www.investopedia.com) is very useful, as it provides basic definitions on a wide range of terms and also gives you links to other resources. Definitions are also provided in the glossary at the end of this book.

Here are some of the terms you need to understand in options trading.

There are two kinds of options. A *call* grants its buyer a right (but not an obligation) to *buy* 100 shares of stock at a specific, fixed price per share before a specific date. Anyone who sells a call grants these rights to a buyer on the other side of the transaction.

A *put* grants its buyer a right (but not an obligation) to *sell* 100 shares of stock at a specific, fixed price per share before a specific date. Anyone who sells a put grants these rights to a buyer of the put.

An option's *premium* is its current value, equivalent to a stock's market price. The premium value is expressed in a shorthand format representing dollars and cents. For example, if an option is listed with a value of 2, that means $200. If the value is 2.25, a single option is worth $225.

Every option comes with a specific *expiration* date. Most options expire within a few months, although a *LEAPS* (Long-Term Equity Anticipation Security) option may extend out as far as 30 months. As expiration gets near, the premium will fall in value. At the end of the expiration day (the third Friday of the expiration month), the option is worthless.

If you buy an option, one of four actions is going to occur before expiration. First, you can *exercise* the option, meaning you will buy or sell 100 shares of stock for each option you own. (Remember that a call entitles you to buy, and a put entitles you to sell.) Second, the option might be subject to *automatic exercise,* meaning that exercise takes place if the option is *in the money.* For a call, this means the market value of stock is higher than the *strike price*; for a put, it means the market value is lower than the strike price. That price is the price at which a specific option can be exercised in all cases. Third, the option might be *out of the money,* in which case automatic exercise will not take place. The option is out of the money when the stock's market value is lower than a call's strike price or higher than a put's strike price. Fourth, the stock's price may be exactly the same as an option's strike price. In this case, the option is *at the money.* These positions describing proximity between the strike price and current value of the stock are all-important because they determine an option's premium value.

Figure 3-1 summarizes in the money, out of the money, and at the money for a call. Figure 3-2 provides the same information for a put.

The names of options are derived from the action occurring upon exercise. For anyone on the *short* side (meaning the option was sold), exercise means stock is *called away* upon exercise of a call, or that stock is put to the short seller upon exercise of a put. Exercise is also called *assignment* because at the time of exercise, a specific call is assigned to a trader. Not all options are necessarily

FIGURE 3-1. CALL STATUS.

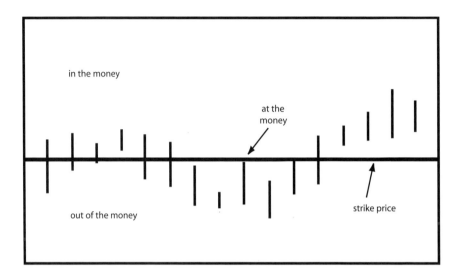

FIGURE 3-2. PUT STATUS.

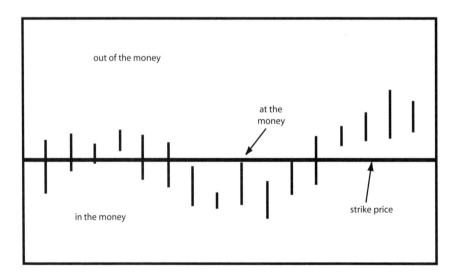

exercised, so assignment occurs when an option owner executes *early exercise* of his or her *long* position (you are long when you buy an option and short when you have sold; this is explained in more detail in the next section).

All options are defined by a series of *terms* that cannot be transferred or changed. First is the kind of option (call or put). Second is the strike price. Third is the expiration month. And fourth is the *underlying security*, the stock to which the option refers. All of these terms are needed to distinguish one option from another. For example, a reference may be made to:

MRK Jul 45 call
MSFT Sep 30 put

These references include all four terms. The first reference is a Merck July 45 call; the second is a Microsoft September 30 put. This sequence includes the underlying security (Merck or Microsoft); the expiration month (July or September); the strike price ($45 or $30 per share); and the type of option (call or put).

Long and Short

Most investors relate easily to the concept of going long. This means you enter a position by first purchasing it, and close the position later by selling. This is the sequence employed for investing in stock as well as for buying real estate and other investments. The long position involves a sequence of transactions. First is a trade described as *buy to open*, which simply means you put money into either shares of stock or an option. Later, when you want to close the position, you enter a trade called *sell to close*. This means the transaction is finalized, and the net difference between the two trades is a profit or loss.

Now imagine this sequence in reverse. A *short seller* initiates a trade to sell at the beginning of the sequence and buy it later to close. When you short stock, it is a complex transaction. You have to first borrow the stock from your broker and sell it, and later, buy to close. The sequence involves payments of interest to your broker as well as a considerable risk. You would short stock in the belief its value is going to fall, but if the value of stock rises, short sellers lose.

The process of going short in options is much less involved because you do not need to borrow an option from the brokerage firm. The act of selling actually creates the option, so it is a simple process. The risk level, however, varies from highly conservative to highly speculative, so before devising a short strategy with options, you need to fully understand the exposure to risk the strategy involves.

A short seller initiates the sequence with an opening *sell to open* transaction. For example, once you sell to open, you receive the premium at that time and it is yours to keep. When you close the short option position, the trade is described as *buy to close*. The net difference between the opening sell and closing buy represents profit or loss.

There are only two basic long positions in options. You either buy calls (in the belief the stock is going to rise), or you buy puts (believing the stock is going to decline). If you are right about the direction of price movement (and if it happens before expiration), your long option position will be profitable. You can sell the long call or put and keep the net profit in the transaction, or you can exercise. When you exercise a call, you are entitled to buy 100 shares of the underlying security at the strike price, even if the current market value is much higher. When you exercise a put, you sell 100 shares of stock at the strike price, an action you would take when the current market value of stock was lower than the put's strike price.

On the short side, there are many variations and strategies worth considering. Remember, some short strategies are high-risk and even inappropriate for inexperienced or conservative traders, while other short strategies are very conservative.

The *covered call* is one of the most popular short strategies. It is also the most conservative option strategy. It involves selling one call per 100 shares you own. In an ideal situation, the strike price of the short call will be greater than your basis in the stock. For example, if you buy stock at $46 per share and later sell a covered call at 50, you will profit in three ways upon exercise. First, you will earn 4 points ($400) from a capital gain on the stock. Second, you keep the option premium you were paid when you sold the covered call. Third, you continue to earn dividends as long as you own the stock (even when you have sold a covered call). If dividends earned during the period were $50, the overall net profit on this covered call and stock transaction would be:

Strike price of call	$5,000
Original cost of stock	4,600
Profit on stock	$ 400
Plus: option premium received	400
Plus: dividends received	50
Total profit	$ 850

In comparison, the *uncovered call* (also called a *naked call*) is very high-risk. The covered call can be designed to produce a profit upon exercise. But in theory, a stock's market value could rise to any level, so the risk associated with an uncovered call is quite high, at least potentially. Risk does not always mean the outcome will occur, however. As previously stated, about three-quarters of all options expire worthless, so even an uncovered call's risk is not absolute. You earn a premium when you sell an uncovered call, so the risk is that the stock's value will rise above the strike price. If it is exercised, you will have to pay the difference between the current market value and the strike price. For example, if you sell an uncovered call with a strike price of 45 and the stock is at $52 by expiration, it will be exercised. If you received $400 when you sold the uncovered call, your net loss (before brokerage charges) would be:

Market value of stock at expiration	$5,200
Strike price of uncovered call	4,500
Loss on stock	$ 700
Less: premium received	400
Net loss	$ 300

Option listings show values in shorthand form. When, for example, the premium value is $400, it is shown as 4. A $45 strike price call expiring in June is described as a "June 45 at 4." The difference between covered and uncovered calls is substantial in terms of risk, which places these two strategies at opposite ends of the spectrum. The covered call is quite conservative, and the uncovered call is the most speculative strategy you can employ.

In comparison, the put can also be sold, but it cannot be covered in a real sense. If you sell a put, it can certainly be used to hedge other stock or option positions, but it is going to be an *uncovered put* with a specific risk level. But that risk level is lower than the level for uncovered calls. With a call, the stock price can (in theory, at least) rise indefinitely. But the same stock's value can fall only so far. The difference between the strike price of an uncovered put and zero is the ultimate risk. But more realistically, the likely worst case scenario for an uncovered put is the tangible book value per share of the company's stock. Even upon complete liquidation of a company, the stock is not going to fall below this level, which represents the net worth of tangible assets. The risk of an uncovered put is the difference between the strike price and tangible book value per share, further reduced by the premium you receive for selling the put.

EXAMPLE

You sell a put with a strike price of $25 and receive a premium of 3 ($300). Tangible book value is $9 per share, so the maximum risk is:

Strike price of the put	$2,500
Less: tangible book value	900
Stock risk	$1,600
Less: premium received for put	300
Maximum risk	$1,300

This does not mean that a short seller of a put will lose $1,300. For example, the put might be exercised when the stock's market value was $2,200, or 3 points below the strike price. In this instance, the loss on stock would be offset by the premium received for selling the put (but not counting transaction fees).

Short selling of calls and puts is more complex than the relatively straightforward process of going long (buying options). However, short sellers always have a time advantage. Anyone who buys options has to be concerned with the passage of time. The closer to expiration, the more the option's premium value declines, so even when stock values remain steady, it is quite possible to experience a loss on a long option position. In comparison, that same diminishing value helps anyone who is short on calls or puts; because the opening transaction is to sell the option, decreased value means the positions can be closed for less money, producing a net profit.

Time is the most important element to consider in option valuation, and the option premium contains three types of value: time value, extrinsic value, and intrinsic value. They are described in the following section.

Types of Value

The option's premium—its total value at any given time— consists of three separate parts. This complexity is what makes options difficult to anticipate, but also most interesting as a portfolio management tool and income generator.

For anyone in a long position, time is the enemy. The closer to expiration, the lower the option's premium, based strictly on the time element. So *time value premium* is that portion of total premium caused strictly by the passage of time. The more time remaining until expiration, the more time value premium is found in the total premium. This is the reason that short sellers have a great advantage. Even if the stock holds its value over a period of months, the option premium is going to evaporate as time value premium moves further downward. The evaporation of time value premium accelerates as expiration comes closer.

What most people call time value premium actually contains a second element not related to time itself. This *extrinsic value premium* reflects the level of interest in the option and the stock, and it changes according to market perceptions about future price changes. For example, if a stock is quite volatile, with a broad trading range and a tendency to move up or down in rapid increments, then extrinsic value premium reflects the volatility as well. This element of premium is usually lumped in with time value premium and can mislead an observer. It would seem logical that time value premium *should* be very predictable. In fact, if you exclude the volatility reflected in extrinsic value, the time-only element of an option premium is quite predictable. Figure 3-3 provides a simplified version of how time value premium changes over time, when you exclude extrinsic value from the analysis.

If you consider *time* alone, the declining value is tied specifically to expiration and will be predictable. The decline accelerates as expiration nears. However, the time value premium usually includes extrinsic value, so its change is a combination of pure time value plus market volatility in the stock.

Whenever an option is in the money, its premium also includes *intrinsic value*, which is the number of in-the-money points. For example, if the current price of a stock

FIGURE 3-3. TIME VALUE PREMIUM—WITHOUT EXTRINSIC VALUE.

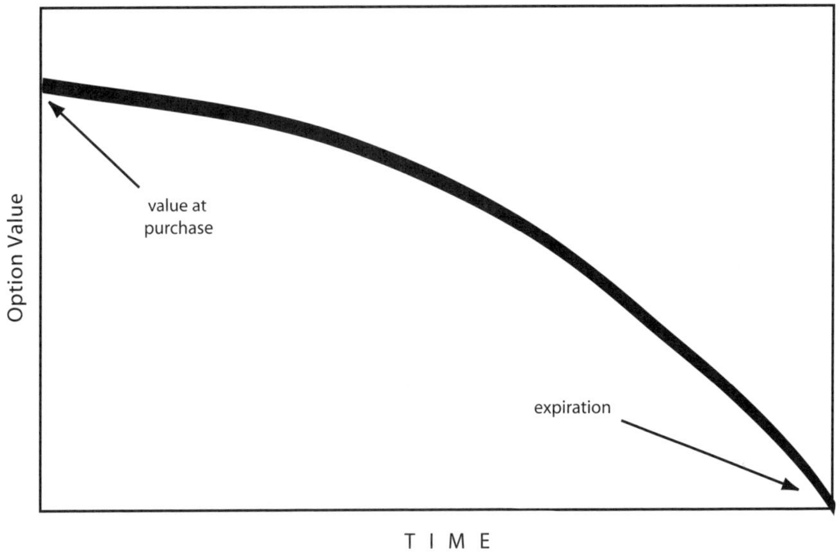

value at
purchase

expiration

Option Value

T I M E

is 3 points higher than the option's strike price, calls with that strike price will contain 3 points ($300) of intrinsic value. If the current price of stock is 4 points below a put's strike price, the put will contain 4 points ($400) of intrinsic value.

Although intrinsic value changes point for point with the stock, you might not necessarily experience overall changes in premium value, because of adjustments in extrinsic value. For example, an in-the-money call might be seen to move 3.5 points although the stock's price rose only 3 points. This means that extrinsic value rose by a half point. This can also work in the opposite direction. For example, stock moves up 4 points but an in-the-money call rises only 3 points. When this occurs, it is a combination of 4 points intrinsic value growth, minus 1 point decline in extrinsic value.

The intrinsic value levels and locations relative to strike price are shown in Figure 3-4. Note that intrinsic value

FIGURE 3-4. INTRINSIC VALUE AND LOCATIONS RELATIVE TO STRIKE PRICE.

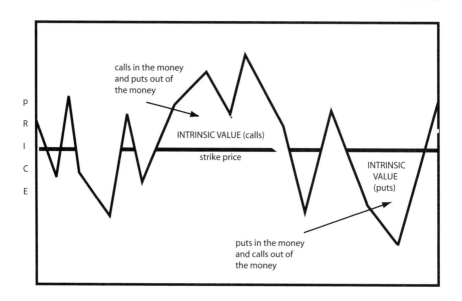

resides on opposite sides of the strike price for calls and for puts. It is above the strike price for calls; in other words, the number of points the stock is above the strike price is equal to the intrinsic value premium. For puts, the opposite rule applies.

If you keep the attributes of the three kinds of value in mind, you will better understand how option valuation works:

- *Intrinsic value* exists only when the option is in the money and is equal to the number of points between the strike price and current market value.

- *Time value* is predictable and is greater when a long time remains until expiration. As expiration approaches, time value declines at an accelerated rate, reaching zero on expiration day.

- *Extrinsic value* reflects volatility in the stock itself and is a pure measurement of the risk/reward factor. Just as a stock with wider trading range (greater volatility) is always going to be higher-risk, options on the same stock will reflect more extrinsic value; and the greater this volatility, the greater the tendency of the option to overreact to changes in the underlying security's price changes.

Moving In and Out of Positions

Just as you buy, hold, and sell stocks, a series of transactions defines the way that options are traded. Because short selling of options is easier than shorting stock, some traders conclude—wrongly—that option trading is more complex than stock trading.

In fact, it is not. There are two general sequences to option trading:

1. *Long:* Buy, hold, sell
2. *Short:* Sell, hold, buy

This is complicated by the fact that exercise or expiration can also occur. This aspect adds four additional possible outcomes:

1. *Long exercise transaction:* Buy, hold, exercise
2. *Short exercise transaction:* Sell, hold, exercise
3. *Long expiration:* Buy, hold, expire
4. *Short expiration:* Sell, hold, expire

When exercise takes place, someone is required to purchase 100 shares of stock or to sell 100 shares of stock at the fixed strike price. If you own a long call, you can exercise it and buy 100 shares of stock at the strike price. Alternatively, if the call is in the money and you take no money, the call may be exercised automatically and the stock is granted to you at the strike price upon expiration. If you own a long put, the opposite transactions occurs. If you exercise, you have the right to sell your 100 shares at the strike price, even if the market value of the stock is much lower.

On the short side, the outcome is quite different. If you have sold a call, exercise means your 100 shares are called away at the strike price. Thus, if it is a covered call, your risk is minimal (assuming you sold a call with a strike price above your original cost). However, if it is an uncovered call, exercise means you have to pay the difference between the strike price and current market value. For example, if your uncovered call's strike price was 40 and the stock is worth $60 per share at expiration, you would have to pay $2,000 (the difference between market value and strike price).

If you sold a put, it means the buyer on the other side has the right to put stock to you (sell it to you) at the strike price. This occurs when the market value is lower than the strike price. For example, if you sold a put with a strike price of 20 and the stock is currently worth $16 per share, you have to pay $2,000 for the 100 shares—even though the current value of 100 shares is only $1,600.

Because the outcomes can take place in many different ways, a variety of potential costs are involved in the exercise of options. Thus, another factor to be aware of is your broker's margin requirement. When you enter an option position, you are going to be required to maintain the minimum margin requirement in your account. For example, if you are required to pay cash for 50 percent of stock you buy, when you sell put, your broker will require you to maintain 50 percent of the strike price. So if the put is exercised, you will have the required margin amount on hand. In some kinds of transactions (like uncovered calls), the margin requirement may change as the underlying security's price moves. Thus, your broker is likely to require you to deposit additional sums if a stock's price moves in a direction opposite of what you hoped for.

Option transactions not only have a variety of possible outcomes but likely consequences as well. The margin requirements are intended to reduce potential losses or at least ensure that you have the resources to maintain federally required margin levels.

Another trading consideration is the level of approval your broker grants to you. Everyone who trades options is required to submit an option application, receive and read the disclosure document, and specify his or her experience in option trading. Your approval level is also based on the dollar value of your portfolio. So unless you are given the highest approval level, you may not be able to execute all types of trades. At the very lowest level, you may be allowed to buy only calls and puts; at the next level, covered calls are allowed; and each subsequent level allows you to execute increasingly complex types of trades within your account.

Learning to Expect the Unexpected

Many first-time stock investors learn from hard experience that things do not always conform to the plan. The same is true in the options market. Novice investors make a mistake in assuming that their entry price is the starting point in a price trend. In practice, that entry price is usually part of an already established trend. You might buy at the bottom, middle, or top in a price range, but if you do not check the trend before entering a position, you cannot know. It is not really looking for the unexpected event so much as doing preliminary research that sets up a successful investment program.

Options are somewhat different from stock investing. Options are intangible *rights* rather than actual shares, units, or properties—and this fact troubles some people. But once you appreciate what those rights include, you will realize that options can hedge other positions to reduce risks and increase current income. However, options also expire. Since options have a finite life, long position option holders have a problem with the time aspect. This problem is an advantage to anyone in a short position, though, and this is the key. Here are some important guidelines for option traders aimed at eliminating the unexpected:

• *For long positions, be aware of time value and time remaining.* Time value is the big problem whenever you buy long positions. Time value is going to evaporate between your purchase date and expiration. For example, if you buy an option at the money when there are six months remaining until the expiration date, and you pay 4 ($400), what does that mean? Even if the option is 4 points in the money on expiration day, that option will still be worth only 4. The time value declines and is replaced by intrinsic value. The net outcome for you is zero gain. Figure 3-5 demonstrates how time and intrinsic value can be exchanged without any gain in an option's long position.

• *For short positions, seek maximum time value and be aware of proximity between the current price of stock and the strike price of the option.* The time value issue is a different matter when you sell options. The evaporating

FIGURE 3-5. THE TRADE-OFF BETWEEN TIME VALUE AND INTRINSIC VALUE.

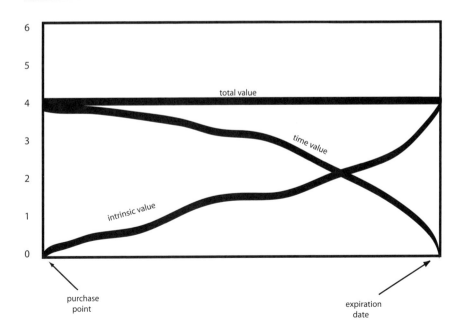

time value is the source for profits, in fact, for the majority of short option positions. Because you initiate the position with a sale and close it later with a purchase, diminishing time value is a benefit. With this in mind, you will increase your profits in short positions by seeking maximum time value in the premium. This is an opposite approach from the one appropriate for the long option position, when time value should be minimized. The greater the time value, the higher the potential for profit.

Of course, high time value is invariably found in options with more time to go until expiration. For highly volatile stocks, the higher extrinsic value may also serve as an advantage because option premium levels are going to be higher. However, the extrinsic value is also a measurement of risk. This is a double-edged sword for short sellers. You want the higher premium, but that also means that there is an increased risk of exercise. In addition to the fact that you might experience exercise, a second issue has to be raised: What is the effect on your portfolio in the event of exercise? If a call, do you want to sell shares of the company involved? If a put, are you willing to buy shares?

• *Before you go short, be sure you are ready to accept exercise.* One of the most basic rules for all options traders involves a willingness to accept exercise. That is always one of the possible outcomes and, while exercise is more common at expiration, it can happen at any time an option is in the money.

Most short sellers are willing to accept exercise as long as they have calculated the outcome of the transaction in its various possibilities. The ideal option transaction is one that produces a profit in all possible outcomes—and especially with covered calls, that is easily accomplished. At the same time, even accepting the possibility of exercise, short sellers are likely to prefer avoiding exercise whenever possible. This is achieved by closing one short position and replacing it with another that expires later, possibly also with a higher strike price. This *rolling* strategy can be achieving profitably in one of two ways. First, you can create a net credit while rolling, which is the ideal situation. Second, looking at the transaction another way, you may accept a small net cost in exchange for more points in the strike price.

EXAMPLE

A covered call was sold for 4 ($400) with a strike price of 35. A few weeks before expiration, the stock was selling for $38 per share, and it was likely that the call would be exercised. Although that would be profitable, an alternative would be to roll the call forward. The 35 call was selling at 6 ($600). Buying to close would create a $200 loss, but it could be replaced with a new covered call with a strike price of 40, expiring three months later and currently valued at 5 ($500). The net in this transaction would be a loss of $100 ($600 buy to close, less $500 sell to open). However, because the strike price of the replacement call is 5 points higher than the original, the net cost of $100 is a reasonable trade for the additional 5 points the trader would earn in the event of exercise.

• *Know the reasons you enter a specific position. With options, you need to know in advance* why *you are using the option.* The most successful strategy is one entered for a specific reason, with exact goals in mind. Of course, every trader wants profitable transactions, but profit is not always an immediate or a direct motive. For example, you can buy puts to protect paper profits in a long stock position after a significant price run-up. That is one of several alternatives. If you are tempted to take profits but you would prefer to keep the stock, you can use options to protect profits or to hedge against market risk. You can also use covered calls to create a low-risk strategy to increase current income—again, without needing to sell stock. Options are perfect vehicles for controlling portfolio positions and reducing risks. But before any strategy is used, you need to know not only the risks but the reasons for going into the strategy itself.

Too often, investors have ill-defined goals or simply do not understand the potential of options. They buy calls and puts without analyzing the stock and its volatility; they sell covered calls at the wrong strike price (so that in the event of exercise, a loss would result instead of a profit); or they create strategies with much higher risks than they can afford. The solution to these problems is to embark on a systematic analysis of any strategy beforehand, to ensure that the range of outcomes is well understood and that all of those outcomes conform with your risk tolerance and meet your investment goals.

• *Come up with a very specific exit strategy, and stay with it.* Option traders may make the biggest mistake of all: failing to set an appropriate exit strategy. This results in a situation where you can never take profits. For example, if you buy an option and it falls in value, you may decide to keep it until it returns to the original price. If it rises in level, you might convince yourself the trend will continue. In this scenario, there is no trigger to take profits or to cut losses.

Any time an option position is open, whether long or short, a specific limit should be set on losses, and a profit target should be set as well. These limits and targets will vary based on the strategy and status of the option. Proximity between current stock price and option strike price defines profit (and loss) potential, which may also affect the limits you set. Time until expiration is also likely to determine the range of potential profit or loss. For example, for a specific strategy, you might set the goal that you will sell when one of two events occurs: the net purchase price is doubled, or it is halved. In this way, you either double your money or lose half of it, so a $200 investment will be turned into $400, or the loss will be cut when the option is worth $100. Each situation should be analyzed on its own merit before a goal is set.

Reading the Options Quotation

Most investors are familiar with the details shown in a stock listing. It includes a 52-week trading range, current yield, trading volume, opening price, closing price, and points gained or lost for the trading day. The options quote is quite different. It provides valuable information, but at first glance it might be confusing.

The typical listing includes not only the specific option and its latest price but also the volume of trades for the day and both the bid and ask prices. The spread between the bid and ask is the difference paid by buyers or received by sellers. Most people who study option listings are interested primarily in the last price traded. A sample of an options listing is shown in Table 3-1.

This table summarizes the closing values for certain calls and puts traded on Citigroup as of the close of April 5, 2007. This was a Thursday and the market was closed the following day for Good Friday. There were two weeks remaining until the April contracts expired, which is reflected in the values of both calls and puts. The first line under "calls" reports that the April 40 call closed at 9.43 ($943). If you add this to the strike price of 40, you arrive at a total of $49.43. The stock closed at $51.57 on this

TABLE 3-1. A SAMPLE OPTIONS LISTING.

Citigroup, April 5, 2007 (closed at $51.57 per share)

Calls		premium	Puts		premium
APR	40	9.43	APR	40	0.05
	42.50	8.90		42.50	0.05
	45	6.60		45	0.05
	47.50	3.90		47.50	0.05
	50	1.95		50	0.25
	52.50	0.40		52.50	1.20
	55	0.05		55	3.80
SEP	40	12.00	SEP	40	0.25
	42.50	9.00		42.50	0.42
	45	7.30		45	0.60
	47.50	5.10		47.50	1.05
	50	3.50		50	1.80
	52.50	2.05		52.50	3.13
	55	1.05		55	4.40

day, so the intrinsic value is below the stock's current market price. The second line under "calls" refers to the 42.50 call, which was at 8.90; added to the strike of 42.50, this came out to 51.40—much closer to the current stock price level.

The exercise of calculating intrinsic value versus closing stock price reveals a lot about trader sentiment about a specific option, especially only two weeks before expiration. With little or no time value remaining in these contracts, you expect the numbers to be close.

The September contracts shown in Table 3-1 are interesting in comparison. The September 40 reports virtually no time value, even though five months remained until expiration. The contract closed at 12 ($1,200). When added to the strike of 40, that came out to $52 per share, and Citigroup closed at $51.57 the same day. In fact, the first four calls in this group showed little or no time value even with five months to go until expiration. With nearly 100 percent intrinsic value, these calls could be good plays for long-side speculators. Since the 40 and 50 September calls have similar value (based on strike plus premium), it would be a far lower risk to buy the 50s at $3.50 than the 40s at $12. The lack of time value in these five-month calls reflects the market pessimism about the company's potential to rise above then-current levels.

On the put side, the first four April contracts were out of the money and showed minimal value of only 0.05 each. The higher the strike prices, the greater the intrinsic value. For example, the 52.50 put was at 1.20. This consists of 0.93 intrinsic value (52.50 less 51.57) and 0.27 time value. The 55 was at 3.80, which included 3.43 intrinsic value and 0.37 time value. It is interesting to note the 0.10 difference in time value between these two puts. Although the time remaining is identical, the time value is not. This means that the put's extrinsic value is 10 cents greater for the 55 put than for the 52.50.

The September puts are valued higher in all cases than the April puts, reflecting the five months' greater time until expiration. It is interesting to observe that the puts in this case are priced with the normal time value expectation, while calls were not. This means that, in the opinion of the market as a whole, Citigroup's prospects for falling value were greater than its prospects for rising value in the next few months.

Each brokerage lists options in slightly different formats, but all contain a wealth of information to help you make judgments about value and bargains. You will find as a general rule that very low-volatility stocks offer very inexpensive options. This is true because there is less likelihood of a big price movement. Citigroup is a moderately volatile stock, and many of the usual signs were encouraging in April 2007, both as a stock investment and for option trading. The stock was midrange in its 52-week trading level, which had been between $46.22 and $57.00. This meant volatility was at 23 percent. At the time, the company was yielding a 4.2 percent dividend, earnings per share was $4.31, and the P/E ratio was only 12.

On the options side, selling covered calls would be quite profitable as well. For example, if you had bought the stock at the closing price, $51.57, and then sold a September 52.50 for 2.05, that would produce a 4.0 percent return in five months (assuming the call expired worthless). This translates to a 9.6 percent annualized return. (To annualize, divide return by the number of months until expiration, and then multiple by 12. In our example, this would be: 4.0% ÷ 5 × 12 = 9.6%.) This annualized return, added to the 4.2 percent dividend, results in an annual yield of 13.8 percent—not a bad return on a stock with a five-star rating from Standard & Poor's (five-star is a "strong buy" recommendation).

Citigroup was selected here to demonstrate how options can be used to maximize your portfolio. This is a highly rated company with exceptionally strong fundamentals; the stock price was moderately volatile (23 percent is not considered high); the dividend yield was quite high, and the P/E ratio very modest. At the same time, options yielded excellent returns, and the combined option and dividend yield were in double digits. Whenever you can locate such safe investments that will yield as well, it makes sense to use options to maximize portfolio returns—with no added market risk.

In Chapter 4, a range of basic option trading strategies are analyzed using real-world examples. These include six basic strategies: long options, covered calls, uncovered calls, uncovered puts, rolling strategies, and insurance strategies.

A PRIMER ON OPTIONS TRADING

"The instability of the economy is equaled only by the instability of economists."
—John Henry Williams, in the *New York Times*, June 2, 1956

SIX BASIC STRATEGIES can help you to work within your portfolio and make profitable use of options. The strategies are (1) long options, (2) covered calls, (3) uncovered calls, (4) uncovered puts, (5) rolling strategies, and (6) insurance strategies. Each has a specific and unique purpose. Understanding the risks of each, the attributes of each, and the trading steps involved in each provide you with the tools you need to structure an option-based portfolio management system.

The purpose in using options is worth mentioning once more: You should focus on the proper selection of stocks as a match for your risk tolerance and long-term goals. That is always the most important aspect in developing a strong investment portfolio. Options can be employed to:

- Take advantage of momentary price movement without needing to sell stock

- Create current income without added market risk

- Speculate, if and when appropriate

- Establish a contingent purchase plan for the near-term future

- Replace a current set of short options with later-expiring contracts

- Provide insurance to protect paper profits against possible downside movement

The six strategies that follow accomplish these specific portfolio-centered goals. These strategies need to be reviewed and studied in the context of managing your portfolio, and in a manner that compares risks among strategies. Ultimately, the purpose of using options in your stock portfolio should be to protect positions and enhance profits. For the typical investor not using options, this normally involves picking stocks intelligently and trying to time your purchase to get a bargain price. However, this is not always possible because market instability may cause short-term price gyrations. Among the many benefits of option planning is that market volatility is not a problem but an advantage.

Basic Long Options

Most people start out with an understanding of the basic purchase of calls and puts. The appeal is that for a very small amount of cash put at risk, potential returns can be rapid and impressive. It is entirely possible to put a call or put for $200 and see it double to $400 in a matter of days or, in some cases, hours. But option investing is not simply a way to double your money; it is more likely a case of "double or nothing."

Three-quarters of all option contracts expire worthless, because of the wasting nature of time value. This means that in about 75 percent of cases, you are going to lose some or all of your money in long options, especially if your use of those options is a purely speculative play. Thus, many investors go to the financial pages or search in their brokerage accounts for long options to buy. This is a backward approach. The generating factor causing you to buy calls or puts is more appropriately based on movement in stocks within your portfolio and not as a method of speculation.

There are two general cases where buying long options makes sense, and both are restricted to stocks you already own. These cases are disciplined approaches to portfolio management, because they are not motivated purely by speculation. Here are the two cases:

1. *The stock's price has risen rapidly in recent trading sessions and you expect a correction.* It frequently occurs that a stock's price rises dramatically after unexpected good news or a broader surge in index levels. For example, a positive earnings surprise, the announcement of a merger or acquisition, or a new product contract may cause a company's stock to rise many points in only a few sessions. This rise is often an overreaction to the news, meaning the price will return to its normal trading range within a few days.

In these instances, you can use puts to take advantage of the temporary surge in price. The temptation at such times is to sell stock—but if your timing is wrong and the stock continues to rise, you lose the opportunity by taking profits too quickly. The alternative is to buy one or more puts at the point where you believe the price has maximized, wait for a return to the normal trading range, and then sell. In this way, you profit from the short-term price swing without having to sell stock. This long put strategy is summarized in Figure 4-1.

2. *The stock's price has fallen sharply on recent news or in response to broader market trends, and you expect the price to rebound.* The opposite effect is often seen on the downside. A stock's price falls below its established trading range as a result of unexpected bad news, a rumor, or broader market trends. For example, a company may announce that it does not expect to meet its current quarter's earnings target. This is not necessarily a sign of bad things to come, but it is likely that the stock price will overreact to the news by falling below its trading range. If you believe that this is a temporary move and you expect the price to return to its established levels within a few days, you can use options to take advantage of the price movement.

FIGURE 4-1. THE LONG PUT STRATEGY OF BUYING PUTS AT THE TOP OF A PRICE RUN-UP.

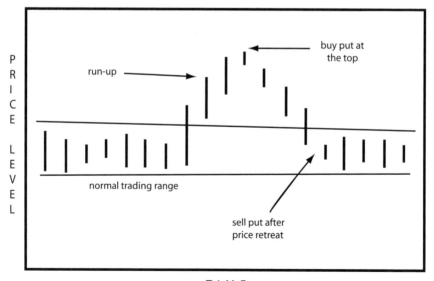

By buying one or more calls at the price point you believe to be the bottom, you will profit when the price rebounds and returns to its establishing trading range. This long call strategy is shown in Figure 4-2.

Note that both of these long strategies are very short-term in nature. Most traders who hold long options over several months struggle with declining time value, often losing money even when the underlying security is level or rising. The two long strategies described above are intended as very short-term, because they are designed to profit from price movement within a few trading sessions. With this in mind, the long strategy makes the most sense when the following guidelines are considered:

- Use options near expiration, because they contain little or no time value. This means they are cheaper and more responsive to the stock's price movement.

FIGURE 4-2. BUYING CALLS AT THE BOTTOM OF A PRICE DECLINE.

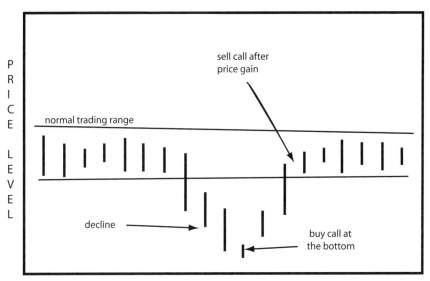

- Buy options in the money but as close as possible to current market value of the stock. This normally means seeking strike prices directly above market value. These are most likely to move point for point in tracking stock price movement.

- Get in and out quickly. Remember, you are trading here on intrinsic value for the most part, and the options will expire within a few weeks, so this is a very short-term strategy designed to take profits and get out.

In Chapter 7, a more detailed strategy using options for *swing trading* provides some specific buy and sell signals for this type of strategy. But there is a difference. Here, the strategy maximizes profits on stocks in your portfolio. Swing trading is meant as a replacement strategy, in which traders seek short-term profits in place of holding stocks as long-term investments.

There is a tendency in using extremely short-term long options to execute a high volume of trades. Because Internet-based trading is affordable, this is not the big problem it used to be, when slight margins of profit were difficult due to trading costs. Today, you can move in and out of option trades for very small commissions. However, it is also important to know the restrictions on *pattern day trading*.

Under federal rules, anyone with open positions traded on margin have to be funded at the end of a trading day. For example, if you are required to keep 50 percent of long positions in your account, that is calculated based on your balances upon the close of trading. But day traders got around this requirement by trading on heavy volume during a single day. By the end of trading, their balances were zero, so day traders figured out how to execute trades on high volume without having any capital in their accounts. To correct this problem, the pattern day trading rule was established.

Under this rule, anyone who moves in and out of the same position four or more times within five consecutive trading days is immediately called a pattern day trader. Under this definition, you are required to keep no less than $25,000 in your brokerage account at all times. If you do not, you are not allowed to continue trading until the shortfall is made up. This has immediate ramifications for option traders, for whom four trades in the same option within five trading days would not be unusual at all. So if you intend to use long puts or calls to take advantage of volatile short-term trading patterns, you might fall under this definition. As long as your portfolio is worth at least $25,000, that is no problem, but if you hold less than that, your ability to move in and out of positions is going to be restricted.

Covered Calls

Using long puts and calls to create profits from short-term overreactions in price is not a high-risk strategy, if only because the amount you put at risk is usually quite small. But if you want a very *conservative* strategy, you probably will end up writing covered calls.

This is the favorite option strategy among conservative investors, because it is possible to enter into a covered call position that will produce a profit in all possible outcomes. It is also possible to accomplish double-digit returns on covered calls with the same low risk that makes it so desirable.

Going short with options is not complicated. You only need to remember that the usual sequence of buy-hold-sell is turned around. When you go short, the sequence becomes sell-hold-buy (or sell-hold-expire or sell-hold-exercise). Some people become confused because they have a difficult time grasping the concept of selling first and buying later. They might ask, "Is it legal?" or "How can you sell something you don't own?

Yes, it is legal. And you *can* sell options as a first step because in doing so, you relinquish a right. This obligates you in case of exercise. By selling the right to someone else, you are giving something up, so the very idea that short sellers are selling something they don't own is not quite accurate. If you sell a call, you are *required* to deliver 100 shares of stock at the strike price if and when the buyer exercises. And if you sell a put, you are *required* to accept 100 shares of stock from the put buyer at the exercise price. So short sellers accept a premium that is theirs to keep; and in exchange, they give someone else the contractual right to either buy shares from them (with a call) or sell shares to them (with a put) at the fixed strike price.

Covered calls are safe because, if properly selected, a profit will result in all possible outcomes. To make sure you pick the right covered call, the strike price should be greater than your original basis in the stock. If you sell a covered call with a lower strike price, exercise would create a net loss, which should not be your goal. For example, let's say you bought 100 shares of stock at $54 per share last month and the stock currently is selling at $52. You sell a covered call with a strike price of 50 and receive a premium of 3. In this situation, exercise means you lose money:

Original cost of stock	$5,400
Less: strike price of covered call	−-5,000
Net loss on stock	$ − 400
Premium received for call	300
Net loss	$ − 100

Given the outcome, why sell the covered call? There is no way that exercise can be profitable, so it simply does not make sense. A better plan is to wait for the stock's price to return to the level close to the original basis, and sell a call with a higher strike price.

What is meant by saying that outcome is profitable in all possible outcomes? Clearly, selling the wrong call (with a strike price below the cost of the stock) is not a wise idea. But if you review calls with a strike price above basis, the possible outcomes (exercise, expiration, or closing the position) all produce profits. Some examples based on stock prices in April 2007 reveal how to analyze covered call outcomes. Two popular stocks on the same option cycle are Exxon-Mobil and IBM. Table 4-1 summarizes available options for these two companies as of April 10, 2007.

Note that for both of these stocks, the current prices reside halfway between the two strike prices selected. To properly select any one of the options shown for covered call writing, you also need to know the original cost of stock. For the sake of this example, let's assume that one month earlier, you had bought 100 shares of each. The Exxon-Mobil shares cost $71.43 (the price on March 13), and the IBM shares were acquired at $96, or slightly lower than the price on the day of the options chart.

The basis in stock is important for two reasons. First, you need to know which option to select to create a true profit in the event of exercise. Second, the calculation of return on covered calls should be based on your actual cost and not on current value. When the return is calculated, the only way to make it comparable among a range of different options is to annualize the return; in other words, it has to be adjusted to show what the return would be if held for one full year. So an option outstanding only one month is annualized if its return is multiplied by 12; a three-

TABLE 4-1. COVERED CALL CHOICES FOR EXXON-MOBIL AND IBM.

Exxon-Mobil, mid-session April 10, 2007
(stock value = $77.57; original cost = $71.43)

Calls		Premium	% (of $71.43)	% annualized
MAY	75	3.60	5.0%	60.0%
	80	0.85	1.2	14.4
JUL	75	5.00	7.0%	28.0%
	80	2.10	2.9	11.6
OCT	75	6.50	9.1%	18.2%
	80	3.60	5.0	10.0
JAN (08)	75	7.70	10.8%	14.4%
	80	4.90	6.9	9.2

IBM, mid-session April 10, 2007
(stock value = $96.38; original cost = $96.00)

Calls		Premium	% (of $96.00)	% annualized
MAY	95	3.50	3.6%	43.2%
	100	0.95	1.0	12.0
JUL	95	4.90	5.1%	20.4%
	100	2.32	2.4	9.6
OCT	95	6.70	7.0%	14.0%
	100	3.90	4.1	8.2
JAN (08)	95	8.10	8.4%	11.2%
	100	5.45	5.7	7.6

month return is multiplied by 4; a six-month return is doubled; and a nine-month return is multiplied by 1.333 (or divided by 9 and multiplied by 12). These calculations are shown for each of the options in the analysis in Table 4-1.

In comparing the two outcomes for any particular month, the apparent disparity between the options can be misleading. For example, you might look at Exxon-Mobil's May options, where the annualized returns are 60.0 percent and 14.4 percent. Why not pick the larger of the two? The problem here is that there is a five-point difference in the two options. So exercise of the May 80 would result in your selling 100 shares of stock for $8,000, whereas the May 75 yields only $7,500. That difference of $500 explains the wide gap in the return on the covered call.

It is not accurate to include the capital gain on the stock in the calculation, as that only distorts the real option potential. However, looking at the overall return with stock included, your calculation would produce far different results:

Exxon-Mobil return if exercised, May 75

Exercise value of stock	$7,500
Less: original cost of stock	7,143
Capital gain	$ 357
Option premium	360
Total profit	$ 717
%	10.0%
annualized %	120.0%

Exxon-Mobil return if exercised, May 80

Exercise value of stock	$8,000
Less: original cost of stock	7,143
Capital gain	$ 857
Option premium	85
Total profit	$ 942
%	13.2%
annualized %	158.4%

Remember, annualizing the return is never intended as a realistic estimate of the kind of return you can expect in every situation. It is only intended for purposes of comparison between two or more strategies. In this example, the annualized return (including capital gain on stock) in the event of exercise is 158.4 percent for the 80 call versus 120.0 percent for the 75 call. The more valid way to analyze these options is to compare strike prices for a range

of months. In the case of Exxon-Mobil, annualized returns
for the 80 options are:

May	14.4%
Jul	11.6
Oct	10.0
Jan (08)	9.2

The annualized return falls as the time is expanded because, with more time until expiration, you have less likelihood of exercise. The May 80 comes up in one month, so
extrinsic value (translation: immediate market interest) is
greater than interest in the farther-out options with the
same strike price. In other words, if Exxon-Mobil were to
move above $80 per share within the following month, the
covered call would surely be exercised. Early exercise for
the remaining covered calls is far less likely.

In selecting covered calls, you have to choose between
the immediate return on the option itself, versus the dollar
amount between calls with different strike prices. For example, the Exxon-Mobil July 75 yielded $2.90 more than
the 80, but if exercised, it would produce $500 less in cap-
ital gain. Another important consideration is the comparison between intrinsic value on the one hand and time/
extrinsic value on the other. In both of these stock examples, the higher strike price options contain zero intrinsic
value and, for covered call writing, this is very desirable.
Remember, time value disappears rapidly as expiration
nears. So for short sellers, higher time value is a positive
attribute.

GUIDELINES: WHEN COVERED CALLS ARE APPROPRIATE

The study and comparison of covered calls has to take into
account a range of judgments about both the stock's price
movement and option values, now and in the future. A

basic assumption is that the stocks you now have in your portfolio are ones you want to hold onto for the long term. So if you are going to write covered calls, that creates one type of risk that you do not have if you simply own shares. That is the risk that your stock will be called away upon exercise.

Many writers of covered calls are willing to accept exercise, but they also try to avoid it through a series of *rolling* techniques. (This is explained later in this chapter.) In quantifying the "lost opportunity risk" of covered calls, what does it really mean? Just owning stock, you always hope the price will rise and you will make a profit. But in selling covered calls, as the previous examples demonstrate, it is entirely reasonable to expect to earn double-digit returns in the highly conservative covered call strategy. Thus, before entering the covered call, you need to decide whether you are willing to take the double-digit return, in exchange for the risk of having your stock called away. Because the exercise of the covered call would produce a profit, that risk is certain. But the alternative, simply holding unencumbered stock in the hope that the price will rise, is not as certain. It does happen, but not every time. So covered call writers create double-digit returns in every case, in exchange for losing the occasional stock whose price went higher than the call's strike price.

Writing covered calls is both conservative and high-yielding. However, it is not always the right strategy. It works when:

- *You are willing to accept exercise.* The most basic test of whether you should write covered calls is tied directly to exercise. You need always to be prepared to have 100 shares of stock called away for each covered call you write. This can occur at any time when the covered call is in the money. It's most common close to expiration, but that does not mean it only happens that way.

- *The option premium makes it worthwhile.* The dollar amount and percentage return from the covered call have to justify the strategy. For example, if a covered call will require you to keep your stock committed for six months for only $85 and with a yield of only 1.2 percent, it might not be worth the trouble. There is absolutely no reason that you should not be able to find annualized returns in double digits with the right stock and the right option.

- *The strike price creates stock profit.* It makes no sense to write covered calls that will result in a capital loss on stock if exercised. The temptation is there because, when you count intrinsic value, the dollar amount of the call is impressive. But when you subtract the net loss on stock after exercise, you are likely to discover that your net return was disappointing. You are far better off limiting your covered call writing to *profitable* scenarios.

- *The outcome is justified.* Rather than focusing only on the return if exercised, also calculate and compare the return if the option expires (called "return if unchanged") and determine in advance when you will close the position. For example, you might decide to close the uncovered call with a "buy to close" order if the option loses half its value. This achieves two benefits. First, it creates an impressive short-term return, enhancing your investment in the stock for no added market risk. Second, it frees you to write another covered call, perhaps one extending out several months longer for more premium and at a higher strike price. Cancellation of a covered call and replacement with another can be continued indefinitely, turning your stock portfolio into a double-digit income generator. When you add together the potential capital gain on stock (in the event of exercise), dividend income, and call premium, the outcome has to justify your decision to use calls. When it does, your portfolio can be transformed into a powerful profit machine.

There are instances in which writing covered calls does not make sense, and your broader portfolio goals and risk tolerance should rule your decisions. These conditions include these scenarios:

- *You will need to sell stock before the expiration of the covered call.* In some situations, it is inappropriate to write covered calls because you will need to close the stock position in the near future. If you commit the stock as cover for a short call, it could create a situation where closing the position creates a net loss.

- *You are uncomfortable about the possibility of losing future price appreciation on the stock.* Some people simply cannot accept the possibility that their stock might rise in value far above the strike price of a covered call. That lost opportunity does not always occur and covered calls easily yield double-digit returns. Even so, you need to accept the chance that some stocks would have outperformed the covered call position, and shares will be called away as a consequence of the covered call. If that possibility is unacceptable, then covered calls are simply inappropriate for you.

- *You do not understand the transaction.* So many losses in the market occur because investors do not understand the risks or do not comprehend the possible range of outcomes. This applies in buying stock as well as trading options. You need to be fully aware of the range of risk and not just the potential profit. If you sell covered calls before you are proficient in the language of options and with the likely outcome—and if you are not sure how to establish an exit point for the strategy—then it is only logical to wait until you have more knowledge. That knowledge and the requisite trading experience can be gained through paper trading (entering a series of transactions in a model portfolio, but without placing any money at risk). One of the best places for paper trading in options is at the Chicago Board Options Exchange (go to www.cboe.com and link to *Virtual Trade Tool* under "Free Tools").

- *The dollar value of calls and percentage return are too small.* Set a minimum dollar value and percentage return (annualized) to make covered calls worthwhile. This helps you to avoid entering positions that are simply not justified. Remember, covered calls can produce annualized yields easily, even when you limit activity to strike prices above your original cost for the stock. There is no need to settle for dismal returns. If you review stocks and find that option yields are too low, that stock might not contain enough price action to justify option trading. This does not mean that you should not buy the stock, but option value may serve as one of many tests you use in picking stocks.

Uncovered Calls

The contrast between covered and uncovered calls is glaring. Covered calls are conservative but high-yielding. Uncovered calls are exceptionally speculative and represent one of the highest-risk trading strategies. For anyone intent on building a long-term and permanent portfolio of value and growth stocks, uncovered calls have no place.

How risky are they? What if you could earn more than $5,500 on an option consisting entirely of time value? Would that justify an uncovered call? Table 4-2 summarizes available calls on Google, a very popular stock.

All of the calls listed are out of the money, so there is no intrinsic value in any of the sample calls. As covered calls, several of these represent potentially profitable candidates. For example, the January 2008 470 call is worth 55.70 ($5,570), which would be an 11.9 percent return on April 10, 2007 values (annualized 15.9 percent). But as uncovered calls, the opportunity is not as exciting.

Table 4-2 indicates that Google ranged, in the six months leading up to April 10, between $445 and $500 per share. Over the previous 12 months, the range was

TABLE 4-2. CALLS ON GOOGLE.

April 10, 2007—Google closed at $466.50 per share

Calls		April 10, 2007 Closing Premium
APR	470	$ 9.90
	480	6.00
	490	3.40
MAY	470	$16.50
	480	12.00
	490	8.40
JUN	470	$21.90
	480	17.00
	490	13.00
SEP	470	$37.50
	480	32.50
	490	28.70
JAN (08)	470	$55.70
	480	49.20
	490	43.20

from $360 to $513—a lot of point spread and volatility.
The point gap in one year was 153 points. If you assume
that the volatility would extend into the future, the possibilities are far from certain. For example, if you wrote an
uncovered January 2008 call at 470, you would receive a
premium of $5,570. But if the stock rose 150 points to
$616 per share, that call would be exercised. You would be
required to deliver 100 shares at $470 per share. Your net
loss:

Assumed market value per share	$61,600
Strike price of uncovered call	− 47,000
Loss on uncovered call	$14,600
Less: premium received	− 5,570
Net loss	$ 9,030

For most people, losing more than $9,000 on a trans-
action is simply beyond risk tolerance levels and unaf-
fordable, so what might look like a very tempting
uncovered call has significant risk attached to it. Stocks
like Google can be exceptionally risky because of volatility
and stock price levels. Even so, the point remains that risks
for uncovered calls are too high for most long-term investors. Uncovered calls also contradict the goals for most
portfolios, which is to find and buy shares of value and
growth companies and invest for the long term. Uncovered
calls might be very profitable in some cases, and catastrophic in others.

An alternative to writing pure uncovered calls is the *ratio
write*. In this strategy, you increase cash income by writing
a grouping of calls, partially covered and partially uncovered. For example, if you own 400 shares of Abbott Labs,
which you purchased at $57.06 per share (the closing price
on April 10, 2007), you could sell five calls. This is a five-
to-four ratio write. The value of the Abbott Labs November

60 calls on that date was $2.10 per share. Selling five calls would yield $1,050. Because this is all time value, the risks are not unreasonable for many investors. With seven months to go until expiration, this ratio write also provides a degree of safety from the $1,050 received in premium.

What happens, however, if the stock were to rise far above the strike price of the covered calls and all five were exercised? For example, if the stock went to $70 per share:

	Covered Portion	Uncovered Portion
400 shares, market value	$28,000	
100 shares, market value		$7,000
Less cost @ $57.06	− 22,824	
profit	$ 5,176	
Plus option premium	1,050	
adjusted profit	$ 6,226	

In this example, the net loss would be $774, because the uncovered portion of the transaction exceeds the capital gain plus option premium. This is truly a worst-case outcome, however, because it assumes that (1) the stock will rise 13 points in seven months, (2) you would not close out one or more calls as time value recedes, and (3) you would not avoid exercise by rolling out of these positions.

Even if this worst-case outcome were to occur, there is a way to eliminate the risk of the ratio write. For example, assuming all of the facts in the example, add one more element: a long November 65 call. On April 10, 2007, that call closed at 0.75. Now the total transaction involves five short calls and one long call, against 400 shares of stock:

4 November 60 calls sold short	$1,050
less 1 November 65 call bought	− 75
Net receipt	$ 975

If all five short calls were exercised, the one long call could be used to satisfy one of those calls, and the 400 shares taken up for the remaining four calls. In this situation, there would be no loss. It would create a net profit of $299 if the stock went to $70:

5 calls sold at $60 per share	$30,000
less: 1 long call at 65	−6,500
Net	$23,500
Basis, 400 shares @ 57.06	−22,824
net loss on stock	$−676
option premium received	975
net profit	$ 299

Using the offsetting long call, a "worst-case" outcome is minimally profitable. However, remember that even this "salvage strategy" might not be necessary; potential losses can be avoided by cashing in one or more calls when time value declines, or by rolling forward to avoid exercise (more on this later in this chapter).

The ratio write can be designed in a number of permutations. For example, you can write one call against 75 shares. You can also write a more conservative version. For example, if you own 500 shares, you can write three covered calls. This leaves 200 shares free of the call obligation and also makes it easier to roll out of a position later on. If you want to avoid exercise, you can close the three short calls and replace them with five later-expiring, higher-strike calls, and the entire transaction can be done with a net credit.

The basic purpose to this strategy is to mitigate risk while maximizing income from call writing. The theory that a stock may rise above the strike price can become reality, however, so the ratio write should be reviewed with market risk in mind. It is a promising potential strategy, especially based on the fact that three out of four options expire worthless. It is that one out of four remaining that you need to think about before entering into any short strategy.

Uncovered Puts

Calls can be covered or uncovered, but puts cannot be covered. When you sell puts, they are uncovered (also called "naked"). Potential losses are limited because a stock can only go down so far. For example, a $20 stock can only go down to zero at the very worst, so the risk is finite. In comparison, a stock could rise indefinitely, so uncovered call writing comes with a theoretical unlimited risk.

The realistic maximum loss in an uncovered put is not as extreme as zero either. The real maximum risk is the company's tangible book value per share. For example, if a $20 stock were to fall to its lowest possible level (assuming, say, complete liquidation of the company), the lowest level per share should be equal to the liquidation value of the company. If the tangible book value were $8 per share, the maximum risk in writing an uncovered put would be 12 points, not 20.

Some investors prefer selling uncovered puts over selling covered calls. If you consider the risk of owning stock, as well as the need to actually put money into shares, you realize that covered call writing does contain risks (even though it is highly conservative). The degree of risk in covered call writing has to be cast with the starting assumption that you already own stock. Thus, you have accepted the risk that the stock's share value could fall in a weak market. The risk of covered call writing is properly compared to simply owning stock and doing nothing. So the risk of being a stockholder is much higher than that of

being a stockholder and writing calls against your portfolio.

Now consider the alternative of selling uncovered calls.
First, you should focus only on stocks of companies you
are willing to own. If an uncovered put is exercised, you
are going to have 100 shares of stock put to you. That
means you will be buying at a price above market value,
since the put will be exercised only when its value is lower
than the strike price. So the actual risk in writing uncovered puts is: *strike price less market value of stock plus put
premium received.*

For example, you sell an uncovered put with a strike
price of 35 and receive a premium of 4 ($400). The put is
exercised when the stock's market value is $33 per share.
Your outcome:

Strike price	$3,500
Less: market value of stock	− 3,300
Loss on stock	$ − 200
Option premium received	400
Net profit	$ 200

The put premium reduces the loss and, in this example,
your real net basis in the stock turns the stock loss into a
$200 profit. You buy shares at $35 when the current market value is only $33, but your real net basis is $31 per
share (because you received $400 for selling the put). Ob-
viously, if the stock's current market value fell below the
net difference in the strike price and current value, you
would have an actual net loss. This is why you should restrict your uncovered put writing to stock you want to
own.

If you compare the two strategies, you might conclude
that the uncovered put is more desirable in some markets
to the alternative of writing covered calls. However, that

comparison may not be relevant, assuming that you want to be long on stock over many years. For anyone who wants to buy and hold stock, covered call writing provides a low-risk method for improving current income for small market risk. Writing uncovered puts works only when you are willing to buy shares of a company but are equally happy to take the income from uncovered puts without the market risk of stock ownership.

Rolling Strategies

All uncovered option positions—covered calls, uncovered calls, and short puts—produce income at the time you open the position. That occurs because of the sell-hold-buy sequence. As the initial seller, you are entitled to receive the premium. This is a great advantage, especially if you are trading solely in time value, because time erodes the premium value, making your short positions profitable.

What happens, however, when the underlying stock's value changes in the opposite direction than you expect? In that case, the option premium level grows too, *after* you have sold the option. As soon as the stock passes the short option's strike price (on the way up for calls or on the way down for puts), the option goes in the money and the chance of exercise becomes a real concern.

It is a paradox that option writers (sellers) are willing to risk exercise, but once in the short position they will probably try to avoid it. This is achieved through a strategy called *rolling*.

When you roll a short option, you take two actions. You close the current position with a closing buy order, and you open a new position in options of the same company. Most rolls move forward, meaning that the expiration time is extended for a longer period of time; this usually produces more income and may create a net credit in the roll. However, a roll can also move backward in time, replacing a later expiration with an earlier one, or roll to a different option with the same expiration date.

For example, you might replace a covered call with a strike price of 40 with a 45 at the same expiration date, and pay a net difference of 2 points. That $200 cost is justified by the 5-point higher strike price. In the event of exercise, your stock is called away at $45 rather than $40.

In cases where two different expiration dates have options with approximately the same value, you might replace a later-expiring short position with an earlier one; accept a small loss on transaction fees; and wait for time value to disappear more rapidly.

Those are unusual situations. Most rolling extends to a later expiration date, and the strategy is usually undertaken to increase income, to avoid exercise, or both. For example, if your 40 covered call is expiring later this month and the stock is currently at $43 per share, you might close your current short call and replace it with a 45 call expiring in three months. That avoids exercise, while potentially creating additional current income or breaking even on the trades. Table 4-3 provides some examples of call values for two companies, Hewlett-Packard and Wal-Mart.

EXAMPLE

You bought 100 shares of Hewlett-Packard at $38 per share and later sold an April 40 covered call. Seven trading days before the April expiration, the stock was at $40.88 per share and you believe the call is going to be exercised. You can roll forward to avoid exercise. If you pick the May 40 call, you will earn 0.80 additional premium on the trade, but the strike price remains at 40. If you pick the September 42.50, you extend expiration to a later date and

TABLE 4-3. CALL VALUES FOR HEWLETT-PACKARD AND WAL-MART

April, 2007—Hewlett-Packard, $40.88 per share

Calls		Premium
APR	40	$1.00
MAY	40	$1.80
SEP	42.50	$1.50

April, 2007—Wal-Mart, $47.88 per share

Calls		Premium
APR	45	$2.65
JUN	45	$3.50
SEP	47.50	$2.85

create only 0.50 additional premium. However, in the event of exercise, you would earn an additional $250 with the higher strike price.

EXAMPLE

You bought 100 shares of Wal-Mart at $44 per share and later sold an April 45 call. Seven trading days before the April expiration, Wal-Mart was selling at $47.88 per share. You want to avoid exercise. You can close the April 45 and replace it with a June 45, which would create additional income of 0.85. Or you could replace it with a September 47.50. This adds more time to the short call and creates only 0.20 in higher premium, probably just enough to cover transaction fees on the roll. However, it also increases strike price by $250.

As you can see from these examples, rolling requires you to make a decision concerning premium levels, time to expiration, and strike price. In theory, you could roll forward indefinitely, tracking a stock as it moves and changes in value, and avoiding exercise indefinitely. This technique is common among covered call sellers.

The same technique can be used for uncovered calls or puts. In the case of uncovered puts, you would avoid exercise by rolling forward and down. As a stock's market price declines, puts become more valuable; so to avoid exercise, you would replace one short put with another expiring later and for a lower strike price. Table 4-4 shows put premium values for the same two companies as in Table 4-3.

EXAMPLE

You sold an uncovered April 42.50 put on Hewlett-Packard. Seven trading days before the April expiration, the stock is at $40.88 and the put is in the money. You consider rolling forward. The May 42.50 is 0.40 higher than the April contract; the August 40 is 0.10 lower, but upon exercise will save $250 (the stock would be put to you at $40 per share rather than at $42.50). The decision should be based on a

TABLE 4-4. PUT VALUES FOR HEWLETT-PACKARD AND WAL-MART.

April, 2007—Hewlett-Packard, $40.88 per share

Puts		Premium
APR	42.50	$1.70
MAY	42.50	$2.10
AUG	40	$1.60

April, 2007—Wal-Mart, $47.88 per share

Puts		Premium
APR	50	$2.15
MAY	50	$2.40
SEP	47.50	$1.95

comparison between extending the same strike price one month, or moving expiration four months forward for a lower strike price.

EXAMPLE

You sold an uncovered Wal-Mart April 50 put. Seven days before the April expiration, Wal-Mart was at $47.88 per share and the put is in the money. To avoid exercise, you review two possible forward roll choices. You can replace the April 50 put with a May 50 for a net 0.25 credit. Or you can replace it with a September 47.50 for a net cost of 0.20. The first choice may avoid exercise by a month and creates a small additional credit but keeps the put in the money. The second involves a small debit but improves potential exercise by 2.50 ($250).

As with calls, put rolling can continue indefinitely or as long as the stock's price continues to fall. Rolling makes sense for the put writer. The original idea is to create income with a willingness to buy 100 shares of stock at the strike price. But if you can later pick up shares of stock at a lower price per share, it is sensible to roll forward and down.

Insurance Strategies

Puts are often overlooked by investors, both on the long and short sides. Far more emphasis is placed on calls, which is a reflection of the usual optimism investors feel toward the market. They buy calls in the belief that the stock's price is going to rise. The possibility that the price might fall is often never brought into the picture—but it happens.

The speculative possibilities of puts have equal weight with calls. Just as calls can be used to take advantage of overreaction to news on the downside, puts can be purchased to ride the wave of optimism on the upside. But a more conservative use of puts has to be mentioned as well: using puts to insure paper profits.

The dilemma every investor faces is what to do when prices rise. Even long-term investors are tempted to take profits when prices move upward, and it is difficult to resist that urge, even when it contradicts your well-defined investing goals. A solution is to use puts as insurance. Say you have paper profits in your portfolio stocks and you do not want to sell for two reasons. First of all, prices might continue to rise. Second, you want to keep the stock and not sell it.

In this situation, you can buy long puts to insure paper profits. If the stock continues to rise in value, the premium you pay for the puts is lost, but if the stock's price falls, the decline in stock value is going to be offset by an increase in the put's value. Those puts can be sold at a profit, replacing the lost paper profits. Table 4-5 shows a range of put values for Kroger. Over six months from October

TABLE 4-5. PUT VALUES FOR KROGER

April, 2007—Kroger, $29.08 per share

Puts		Premium
JUL	25	$0.15
	30	1.65
OCT	25	$0.45
	30	1.80
JAN (08)	25	$0.50
	30	2.10
JAN (09)	25	$1.10
	30	2.50

2006 through April 2007, this company's stock rose from about $23 per share to just over $29 per share. Had you bought shares six months prior and wanted to continue holding them, you might consider using puts to insure your paper profits.

The decision about which put to buy for insurance is a balance between premium level and time. The longer you can have the insurance in effect, the better. For example, in Table 4-5, compare the October 25 to the January (2008) 25. The later put provides an additional three months' insurance, but it costs only 0.05 ($5) more.

The 30 puts in this case are all in the money, so they will tend to track the stock close to a dollar-for-dollar movement. If the stock's value were to fall, the loss would be offset by rising values in the 30 puts. However, the 25 puts, while out of the money, are much cheaper. You can buy long-term insurance at much lower cost. You might look at the gap between strike price and current market value as a form of "coinsurance" and accept the mitigated risk in exchange for lower premium levels.

You can also use put insurance to create potential additional profits. For example, say you may want to continue holding Kroger stock for the long term, but you are concerned about the risk of price decline over the next year. You might decide that the January (2008) 25 puts are the best-priced among those shown in Table 4-5. Although you own 100 shares, you might also decide to buy three of these puts. If Kroger's stock were to fall below $25 per share during the following nine months, these puts would increase in value by 3 points for every point of stock price decline. Thus, you can combine insurance with speculative play. In the event of a price decline, you would not only replace lost value in the stock but also create three times the profit from long puts.

It is clear that options provide you with a broad range

of possible strategies. Some are very conservative and others are quite speculative. As long as the strategies you select serve the interests of your portfolio and match your risk tolerance and personal goals, options can provide you with a far more interesting and profitable approach to investing. In Chapter 5, the lowest-risk strategies are examined in detail, demonstrating how you can vastly improve your portfolio's performance while reducing market risk.

SPREADS AND STRADDLES

"The trouble with facts is that there are so many of them."
—Samuel McChord Crothers, *The Gentle Reader*, 1903   .

OST PEOPLE MANAGING THEIR OWN PORTFOLIOS focus exclusively on stocks. When you add a range of possible option trades to the picture, you transform a two-dimensional portfolio into a three-dimensional machine for producing profits. If this machine is managed properly, you can better manage risks with options than with stocks alone—and this is the primary argument favoring options.

Going beyond the basic strategies of selling covered calls or using long options to take advantage of short-term price movement, you can create a rather sophisticated series of option trades to make your portfolio more than just a group of stocks. Using spreads and straddles, you can discover a world of greater potential within your portfolio. Here are a few cautionary points about these advanced strategies:

- *You need to assess risks before opening any new positions.* The more complex a strategy, the more important it is to understand the risks. For example, a short position can be protected by an offsetting long position. However, if you close the long position, the remaining short becomes an *uncovered* position, which means that a no-risk position immediately becomes a very high-risk one. Getting caught in that position without realizing it can be very costly.

- *Study and be aware of all* possible outcomes. Complex strategies are often appropriate, but you need to analyze all of the possible outcomes that might occur. A mistake some novice option traders make is to concentrate only on the potential of the most desirable outcome while ignoring other possible events (such as net losses).

- *When potential profits are small, it makes no sense to open option positions.* Among the problems of more advanced strategies is the possibility that potential profit is going to be limited. In the interest of hedging against losses by creating offsetting positions, it is common that limited losses also create limited profits. There is no sensible reason for opening a position if the maximum benefits are too small.

Two primary types of advanced strategies are the *spread* and the *straddle*. Either of these can enhance portfolio profits and reduce risks. Both can be modified so that more weight is given to one side than to the other, and both can be designed to create more profits, but invariably with greater risks as well. The rest of this chapter explains the basic spread and straddle designs and variations of those designs.

The Spread

While covered call writing is a safe and profitable strategy, it often creates a problem. For example, if you write a call against 100 shares of stock and that stock subsequently rises in value, the net change in your portfolio is offset by the two positions. Your long stock rises, but in-the-money short calls shadow that rise. Because they are short, greater value for the short call represents lower opportunity to close at a profit, and a greater likelihood of exercise. That is an acceptable outcome. But at the same time, you want to avoid exercise if possible, through rolling forward and up.

Using spreads can also affect the outcome. Rather than a straight covered call strategy, the spread enables you to manage your portfolio to create additional profits if and when the stock moves in a particular direction.

A *spread* is the opening of two or more positions using options on the same stock. They will have different strike prices or different expiration dates. Some spreads will have both of these features. A spread may also be long or short. A long spread involves purchasing two or more options, and a short spread is defined by the sale of options.

When you open a spread with different strike prices but the same expiration, it is called a *vertical spread* (also called a money spread). A spread with the same strike price but different expirations is called a *horizontal spread*. A spread often comes into effect in stages. For example, you might open a covered call position and later modify it with an additional option, creating a spread.

EXAMPLE

A covered call framed in a vertical spread shows how you can plan for price movement of the stock. Table 5-1 provides call values for Bank of America in mid-April 2007. This range of values opens up several spread possibilities. First, looking at covered calls, the August 50 is worth 2.40 ($240), which if exercised would represent a 4.8 percent return in four months (2.4 ÷ 50.40), or 14.4 percent an-

TABLE 5-1. CALL VALUES FOR BANK OF AMERICA.

April, 2007—Bank of America, $50.40 per share

Calls		Premium
AUG	50	$2.40
	52.50	1.20
	55	0.45
NOV	50	$3.10
	52.50	1.90
	55	0.50
JAN (08)	50	$3.50
	52.50	2.20
	55	1.30

nualized. This is a very promising yield. At the same time, the stock is currently 40 cents higher than the strike price of the call. As long as this price remains at or below the strike price of 50, the option will not be exercised. But if the stock rises above that level, the short call would be exercised and the stock would be called away at $50 per share—even if the stock's value was far greater.

The solution is to enter not simply a covered call, but a spread. For example, you could sell the August 50 call for 2.40 and at the same time buy the August 55 call for 0.45. The net credit would be 1.95, or a 3.9 percent return (11.7% annualized). This is based on the assumption that the stock would be somewhere between $50 and $55 per share by the August expiration. But if the stock were higher than $55 per share, the 55 call would produce greater profits.

Even more opportunities are presented by opening a *diagonal spread*, which is a spread with different expirations and strike prices. In this example, you could sell an August 50 for 2.40 and buy a November 55 for 0.50. The net cost would be 1.90, or 3.8 percent (11.4 percent annualized, only fractionally less than the previous spread). The

November 55 is only five cents more expensive than the August 55, but it provides three more months until expiration. Now the situation is very different. For example, whether or not the short August 50 call were exercised, the long November 55 call remains open for an additional three months.

COMPARING SPREAD PATTERNS

The three types of basic spreads—vertical, horizontal, and diagonal—are defined by the differences in both strike price and expiration. Each is suited to a particular strategy. Remember, with spreads you can combine long and short, calls and puts, *and* variations of strike and expiration. The three patterns are summarized in Figure 5-1.

Some strategic comparisons will help further clarify precisely when and where each of these types of spreads might be used within your portfolio. The vertical spread like the one in the Bank of America example (in Table 5-1) demonstrates how a covered call can be modified. Since the "worst case" for a covered call was a double-digit profit, there was no actual flaw in the strategy itself. However, with the stock called away, covered call writers have to be concerned with the lost additional profit potential. In other words, if you had not written the covered call at 50, you would have benefitted *if and when* the stock rose far higher. In the example, the middle zone between $50 and $55 per share represents the area where the vertical spread is not effective. Within that price zone, the covered call would be exercised, but the long call would be worthless. If the stock rose above $55 per share, the long call would be profitable, so you could recapture some profit even with the stock called away.

We used an example of the diagonal spread with Bank of America to show how this strategy is made more advan-

FIGURE 5-1. SPREAD PATTERNS.

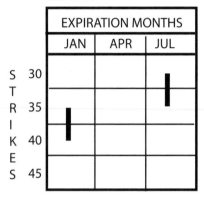

VERTICAL

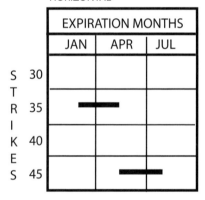

HORIZONTAL

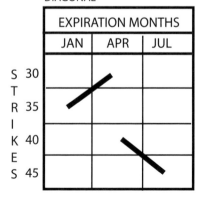

DIAGONAL

tageous. It often happens that an idea is good but the timing is bad. In the options market, that is the definition of a strategy gone bad. But with the diagonal spread, the expiration of the long position is extended three months ahead. It then becomes conceivable that the short side would be exercised in August, but the long side would move into profitable territory before the November expiration. If this concept were extended into the January calls, you would gain six months of "potential time" with the same diagonal spread.

The horizontal spread places yet another variation on the covered call. For example, referring again to the Bank of America case (Table 5-1), if you assume the stock's price per share is going to rise in the next nine months, you can use time value to increase current income, write a covered call, *and* profit from the rising stock value. For example, you could enter a horizontal spread using 50 calls. If you were to buy an August 50 for 2.40 and sell a January (2008) 50 for 3.50, your net credit would be 1.10, or 2.2 percent (2.9 percent annualized). This is a relatively modest return, but it creates an interesting spread play. You might hesitate to pay $240 for a call, slightly in the money, that expires in four months—unless you believe the stock is likely to rise during that time. Even so, most calls expire worthless, so simply going long on this call would be a relatively risky strategy. At the same time, you might hesitate to write a covered call extending out so many months. But the combination of the shorter long position and the extended short position makes more sense.

By the time the August 50 call expires, one of two scenarios is likely. First, it is in a profitable position, so it can be closed for additional current income. Second, it has lost value because the stock has not moved in the money (or not enough), so the call is closed at a loss or allowed to expire. At the same time, the short January call will have also lost value and could be closed at a profit. (In the case of the short call, a closing buy would be available for a smaller premium than the original sale.)

Remember, spread patterns can be entered to mitigate potential future losses, but they also mitigate your profits. In all of these examples, the profit of the covered call is reduced by also entering a long position in the stock. The intention is to profit from a future upward price movement, but it is also possible that both the long and short positions will lose value in the future. If you enter a spread in place of a covered call, you may create greater profits as long as the stock behaves in a particular manner and in the right time frame. But the spread also reduces your potential profit.

Many spreads are entered in increments rather than with both sides opened at the same time. For example, if you write a covered call, you are ready to accept exercise. But after the stock rises and the short call is in the money, you might also see an opportunity to recapture some of the extra value by entering a long position in the same stock. The same can happen when the reverse price direction occurs. For example, you sell a covered call and the stock's price falls. Considering the covered call by itself, you can simply wait out the time value, expecting the short call to expire worthless. But the reduced price might also be temporary. If you expect the price to rebound, you can buy a call, which creates a spread. When the stock's price rises, the long call can be sold at a profit. As long as the cost of the long call is less than what you received for the short covered call, the net credit may justify this position, especially if you would not consider buying options purely on price speculation.

DEBIT AND CREDIT SPREADS

The credit spreads shown in the previous examples are desirable because cash flows into your account rather than leaving. Most option traders recognize that the basic problem with going long is time value. The reason most options expire worthless is that time value evaporates. Thus, you don't just need the option to move in the money; you also need to gain enough in-the-money points to *exceed* the time value premium.

The credit spread, any spread creating higher premium than cost, for this reason, is invariably more desirable than its opposite, the debit spread. For example, in the case of Bank of America, you could create a debit spread as part of a covered call strategy. Referring again to Table 5-1, you could sell an August 55 call and at the same time buy a January (2008) 55. This would result in a debit of 0.85. This strategy would make sense if you believe that in the short term, the stock is not going to rise above the level of $55 per share; thus, the short August 55 call would be likely to expire worthless. However, the January (2008) 55, which expires nine months later, will become profitable if the stock exceeds that strike price. If your timing is off and the August 55 call is exercised, the January (2008) 55 would also be valued at a higher level; thus, you could take profits by selling that call.

The debit spread, any spread creating lower premium than cost, involves problems of time value in the same way that any long position does. In the debit spread example above, the in-the-money premium (all time value) is reduced by the proceeds of the short call. This difference gives you a price and a time advantage.

You can also create either credit or debit spreads outside of a modified covered call strategy. And you can also use puts, either in combination with calls or offsetting each other.

THE UNCOVERED CALL "COVER"

You can use the spread to eliminate the risk of an uncovered call. The strategy is designed to create income from the short call premium, but without the market risk normally associated with uncovered calls.

EXAMPLE

In the case of Bank of America, you can sell an uncovered August 50 call for 2.40 ($240) and at the same time buy a November 55 for 0.50 ($50). The net credit would be $190. If you simply wrote an uncovered call, your risk is substantial. But with the long call attached in the spread, that risk is narrowly defined. The maximum risk in this position is $310 (strike price of 55 on the long side, minus 50 on the short, less net credit of $190).

Long side	$5,500
Less: short	5,000
	500
Less: credit	190
Maximum risk	310

But why would you enter a spread with this level of risk?

First of all, as a means for portfolio management, uncovered calls generally make no sense. They are too risky and provide less current income than most people can afford. But when you consider the leverage involved in this uncovered spread, it makes more sense. For example, you might want to buy 100 shares of Bank of America at its current price of $50.40 per share, but you lack the funds to do so. One solution is to buy a call, but because this is overly speculative, you would prefer a safer strategy. By entering into the spread described above, you accomplish three things. First, you reduce the risk of the uncovered call to a finite level of $310. Second, you create the short-term credit of $190, which will be yours to keep if the short call is not exercised. Third, if the short call is exercised, you can satisfy the assignment with your long 55 call, and your loss will be $310.

Now consider the advantage in the longer term if the short call is *not* exercised. Remember, your purpose is to be able either to buy shares of Bank of America or to profit from the call. If the short call is not exercised, the $240 is yours to keep; but you still own the long call. If the stock's price rises above the $55 per share level before expiration, you can exercise your call and buy shares at $55 (your actual basis would be only $53.10 per share because of your credit spread). You can also sell the 55 call at a profit, further enhancing your income from the spread.

SPREADS USING PUTS

You can also use puts to create spreads. If you believe a stock's market price has risen too far too quickly, buying puts accomplishes the same thing as short calls. If and when the price of the stock retreats, in-the-money puts will increase in value. But if you believe a stock's price has fallen too far too quickly, you can also sell puts, which accomplishes the same thing as buying calls. The advantage, however, is that when you sell puts, you receive cash instead of paying it out. Of course, you can also offset long and short put positions in a spread, depending on what you are trying to accomplish.

The Put Debit Spread

The net debit spread in puts will become profitable if the underlying stock's price falls. Remember, puts increase in value as stock prices move in the opposite direction. Thus, buying puts makes sense if and when you expect the stock price to move south.

As a portfolio management tool, buying puts makes sense as a means for insuring current profits, or merely to speculate on the short-term price swings of the stock. In either case, you do not need to sell shares of stock to earn a profit; puts are well suited to profit taking when prices move too quickly. For example, a favorable earnings report could cause an overreaction in the stock's price. When a stock moves up rapidly on news like that, there is a good chance it will give back some of the gains in the days that follow.

EXAMPLE

If you believe that Bank of America was too high at $50.40, you could use puts to profit from a reversal in price. Some of the company's put values as of April 2007 are shown in Table 5-2.

A put spread resulting in a debit (more money paid out than received) would result if you sold an August 52.50 for 3.10 and bought a November 52.50 for 3.50. The net cost of 0.40 ($40) before trading costs may be worthwhile

TABLE 5-2. PUT VALUES FOR BANK OF AMERICA

April, 2007—Bank of America, $50.40 per share

Puts		Premium
AUG	50	$1.65
	52.50	3.10
	55	5.10
NOV	50	$2.40
	52.50	3.50
	55	5.00
JAN (08)	50	$2.82
	52.50	4.00
	55	5.50

in some situations. Specifically, if you believe the stock's price will move upward in the short term (above the 52.50 strike price), but is likely to decline below that level before the November expiration, this speculative but relatively low-cost debit could make sense. If you own stock in your portfolio, this would be one way to take profits without selling the stock. If your timing is wrong and the August 52.50 was exercised, you could apply the November 52.50 to satisfy it. Your maximum loss in this example is only $40, but the potential gain could be much higher if you are right about the direction of the stock movement and the timing of changes in the price.

The Put Credit Spread

The opposite of a put debit spread is a put credit spread, one in which you receive more money than you pay out. As a strategy for insuring paper profits in your portfolio, the credit spread is a sensible strategy in many situations.

A problem with the strategy of buying a put to insure paper profits is that you have to pay for the put. And the longer until expiration, the greater the cost is going to be. But you can achieve the same insurance to some degree *and* create a credit at the same time. For example (referring to Table 5-2), if you own Bank of America at $50.40 but bought it originally at $45 per share, you might be concerned about the loss of paper profits if the stock's value falls. One way to insure for the short term is to buy an August 50 put for 1.65 ($165). If the stock's value falls below $50 per share before expiration in August, the put can be sold at a profit to offset the paper loss. However, you face the problem of the put's cost, versus declining time value. A solution can be found in the credit spread.

EXAMPLE

You could buy an August 50 put and, at the same time, sell a November 50 put for 2.40. The credit would be 0.75 ($75). This provides you with downside protection for the next few months, plus a net credit. The strategy makes sense only if you are willing to buy additional shares at $50 per share; in the event the short put is later exercised, you will be required to purchase that stock, even if the market price is well below $50 per share. The risk may be worth it to you, assuming two points: (1) you are worried about short-term price decline, and (2) you would be happy to buy another 100 shares at $50 per share if the short put were exercised.

MODIFYING THE SPREAD PATTERN

The previous examples assume you buy and sell the same number of options on either side of the transaction. But spreads become far more interesting when you vary the number of options involved.

For example, you can do any of the following:

- Sell more calls than you buy (profitable when the stock price declines)

- Buy more calls than you sell (profitable when the stock price rises)

- Buy more puts than you sell (profitable when the stock price declines)

- Sell more puts than you buy (profitable when the stock price rises)

You can also combine calls and puts together in various permutations on both the credit and debit side to create even more interesting spreads. Selling both calls and puts at the same time, buying both sides at the same time, selling calls and buying puts, or selling puts and buying calls are all variations of pattern modifications.

As with all option strategies, the complex spread can end up offering limited income potential and exceptionally high loss potential, at times for little or no cash at the time a strategy is opened. Be aware of the dangers in following the apparent logic to a strategy and losing sight of what you are trying to accomplish. If your goal is to improve portfolio profits and reduce risks, complicated spread strategies are probably not going to be as effective as a relatively simple, straightforward strategy. For example, if you are trying to increase current income, compare all strategies to the simple covered call. In many cases, you will come to the conclusion that the less complicated alternative makes more sense.

The various modifications are worth considering, however, in many situations. Any spread can be modified in many ways. A *calendar spread* refers to any spread with options having different expiration dates. A *ratio calendar spread* involves not only different expiration dates for each side of the spread but also a different number of options. For example, you can combine three short calls expiring in August with two long calls expiring in November. Let's look at the positions for Bank of America for some examples.

EXAMPLE

You own 100 shares of Bank of America and you are thinking about selling a covered call. The August 50 is worth 2.40 ($240). However, you also believe that after August, there is a chance the stock's value could rise. The challenge is to create a position that ends up with a net credit but also positions you to benefit if the stock rises before the November expirations. You sell three August 50 calls and receive a premium of 2.40 each (total $720). You also buy two November 52.50 calls at 1.90 each (total cost $380). Your net credit is $340.

In this example, the offsetting long and short positions create cover. If the August short calls are exercised, you can use the November long calls to satisfy the position, and risk is limited to 2.50 points for each. If the August 50 calls expire worthless, you keep the money *and* you have two November long calls. The benefit to this ratio calendar spread is that risks are limited, but you end up with long positions even while creating a net credit in the overall position. As a means for portfolio management, this allows you to use the covered call to create potentially more profits without more cost, and with very limited levels of risk. You could exercise the 52.50 calls if the stock were to rise above those levels, buying an additional 200 shares. Or you could sell them at a profit. If the stock remains below $52.50 per share, the position will still be profitable.

A ratio calendar spread can also be created with puts. For example, in the case of Bank of America, you could sell two August 50 puts for 1.65 each and receive premium of $330. At the same time, you could buy one January (2008) 50 put and pay $282. Your net credit would be $48. The advantage to the position is that one of the short puts is offset by the later-expiring long position. If the short puts expire worthless, you still have a put lasting nine months, which will become profitable if the stock's value falls below the 50 strike price level.

Another variation of the ratio calendar spread involves a combination of calls and puts in the same overall position. When this kind of spread is created, it is called a *ratio calendar combination spread.* However, in studying the combined limitations on both profit and loss of such positions, it usually makes more sense to simply write a covered call or to review the possibilities in a ratio write. Those usually involve about the same level of risk without the complexity of more exotic spread patterns.

The Straddle

While the spread involves the opening of positions above and below the strike price, the *straddle* is created when you buy and sell options with identical strike price and expiration date. The idea behind the straddle is that the offsetting positions will become profitable in some fashion. If you buy a call and a put with the same strike price, one of them will end up in the money. Based on the price movement of the stock, it is even possible that both of them will become profitable. You can also sell a call and a put with the same strike price. You would expect at least one of these options to be exercised, but you depend on the premium credit to create a profit. To write a short straddle, you must be willing to accept exercise on either side of the transaction. This would be an unusual situation with one notable exception—called a *contingent purchase*. In Chapter 6, you will see how a short straddle can be used in a contingent purchase strategy.

Here's how a long straddle works. You have been tracking Bank of America and you decide to open a straddle. You buy an August 50 call for 2.40 and an August 50 put for 1.65. Your total cost is $405. In this position, you need to generate a profit in one of three ways:

1. The call value rises high enough to offset the overall cost of $405.

2. The put value rises high enough to offset the overall cost of $405.

3. Both options become profitable at different times in the period before expiration. The call's value must be greater than 2.40 and the put's value must be greater than 1.65.

These possible outcomes may seem unlikely given the short term involved. Based on the previously established examples with an April stock price, this strategy leaves you only four months for the outcome to turn positive. Because the stock at the time was at $50.40, the vast majority of cash in this straddle represents time value.

A long straddle such as this would seem more reasonable if more time were left. For example, you may buy a January (2008) 52.50 call, which costs 2.20 and has nine months to go until expiration, and also buy a January (2008) 52.50 put for 4.00. Your total cost for this straddle would be $660. So reviewing the strategy, one or both options would have to create more than the 6.6 points in order to break even, and more to become profitable.

A long straddle is a difficult strategy because the requirements are so high. It assumes that price movement will be substantial in one direction or the other. However, most stock market observers would agree that option speculation makes more sense when you decide which price direction is more likely. As a portfolio management strategy, you could justify a long straddle with one argument: You want a combination of the two options to satisfy two concerns. First, if the stock price rises, you would like to be able to buy another 100 shares at the straddle's strike price, but you do not have the cash available today to increase your holdings. Second, you want to protect existing paper profits and buy the put for insurance. Even with this two-part goal, the straddle is quite expensive. It is also contradictory, an attempt to cover all possible bases. The long straddle buyer may be convinced that the $660 cost is justified because it becomes profitable when the stock moves in either direction. The logic is questionable, but the decision to spend money on a long straddle is the individual's choice.

The short straddle is more interesting because it presents a different cash position and an entirely separate set of risks. Chapter 6 presents a strategy that employs either a short spread or a short straddle; for now, the focus is on the appropriate uses of short straddles within your existing portfolio.

EXAMPLE

You may decide to open a short straddle in Bank of America, selling a November 50 call for 1.90 and a November 50 put for 3.50. You receive $540 for the short straddle. If you do not own any shares of Bank of America, this is a high-risk strategy. The uncovered call by itself would be considered a risky decision; when you augment the strategy with an uncovered short put, the danger increases. This makes the uncovered call side of the straddle inappropriate for most people.

However, if you own 100 shares of Bank of America for each call sold in a straddle, the risk level declines considerably. In fact, the straddle then becomes a viable cash generator. For example, if you are willing to purchase an additional 100 shares of the company at $50 per share, you can (1) buy those shares, or (2) sell a put. The short put produces income of $350, which reduces your basis in the stock by 3.5 points if and when the put is exercised. In this case, your net cost for the stock is reduced to $46.50 per share. This makes the straddle reasonable, considering that the short call is covered by the stock you already own. But the key here is that you must be willing to accept exercise in exchange for the $540 you receive. Based on the price of stock of $50.40 per share, this is a yield of 10.7 percent in seven months (18.3 percent annualized). Exercise can occur in the short call or the short put—or in both, based on upward and downward movement of the stock. If both options are exercised, you end up exactly where you were before writing the straddle: owning 100 shares of stock, but $540 richer.

Another aspect to consider in the above example is if the put is exercised. You begin with the assumption that having another 100 shares of the stock at the net basis of $46.50 per share is desirable. Then what do you do with the position after exercise? Looking at the portfolio management aspects of the short straddle (involving a covered call and an uncovered put), the main criticism should be that the exercised put results in buying shares above market value. This is true. However, the 50 strike reduces actual cost of the stock to $46.50 per share, so if the stock is priced between $46.50 and $50 per share, the exercise creates a positive outcome and not a negative. If the stock's value is lower than the net basis, the way to recover the paper loss is through writing subsequent covered calls. The selection of a strike price should be based on the overall basis of the stock. For example, if you purchase 100 shares at $50.40 per share and acquire an additional 100 shares at $46.50, your average basis is $48.45 (not counting the premium of $190 that you previously received for the short call side of the straddle).

Given these facts, you could write calls at or above the strike of 50. If those calls were exercised, the outcome would be profitable. You could also augment earnings by writing yet another short straddle, this time involving 200 shares on each side instead of 100 shares. This increases your risk of having an additional 200 shares put to you below market value, but if your analysis of the company identifies a specific price support level for the stock, you may also conclude that a continued price slide is unlikely.

The short straddle opens up numerous possibilities. However, it is crucial to make a distinction between short straddle *speculation* and short straddle portfolio management. Your willingness to accept exercise of call, put, or both is essential to make the strategy a good fit. And because you probably do not want to carry unreasonable speculative risk, the short straddle makes sense only if the call side is covered. In this way, you maximize premium income and the risk—of having stock put to you—would be a welcome outcome.

The short straddle also can be rolled forward to avoid exercise or, if exercise does occur later, to enhance income at the same time. For example, the short straddle on Bank of America combined a November 50 call with a November 50 put. If the stock rose so that the November 50 call was in the money, that call could be closed and replaced with a forward roll to a January (2008) 52.50 call, or even to a January (2009) 55. In both cases, the roll would be likely to create a net credit.

The same argument applies on the downside. If the stock price fell below the 50 strike and the put was likely to be exercised, a roll forward and down would accomplish the same avoidance of exercise. The short 50 put could be closed with a buy order and replaced with a 47.50 put expiring later, or with a 45 put. In both cases, exercise is avoided and a credit is likely, but you keep the short positions open for a longer period of time.

This is a good example of how option traders are willing to accept exercise and, at the same time, take steps to avoid it. The avoidance of exercise itself is not the sole purpose in rolling forward. Ideally, if you trade for a higher call strike price or for a lower put strike price, you create additional profits in the event of exercise. This justifies the additional time involved. Most people are happy to create additional income in their portfolio using short options, as long as exercise is acceptable and the positions can be rolled to create more premium income and better stock positions in the future.

In Chapter 6, short spreads and straddles are the tools for one of the most interesting option strategies, the contingent purchase.

THE CONTINGENT PURCHASE PLAN

The shortest and best way to make your fortune is to let people see clearly that it is in their best interests to promote yours.
—Jean de La Bruyère, *Characters*, 1688

MOST INVESTORS MAKE A CONSCIOUS SEPARATION between their stocks and options. They *invest* in stocks and they *trade* options. In this chapter, you will discover a series of strategies that work to integrate your portfolio management technique so that you can view option trades as a method within your portfolio and not as a separate activity. Options provide many risk-reducing and income-enhancing strategies. However, option strategies do not have to be thought of outside of your stock portfolio. To be more effective in managing your stocks, you can maximize the power of options by employing them as part of your overall portfolio strategy.

The concept of *contingent purchase* is one that is foreign to many investors. Either you buy or you do not. You buy, hold, and sell. You cannot have it both ways. With options, however, you can lock in a price per share for stock without necessarily buying at all. With the proper application of several contingent purchase strategies, you can have much greater control over your portfolio.

It often happens that investors would like to buy shares of a particular company right now, but they do not have the funds available. The opportunity is lost. In addition, even if you do have the funds, how much risk are you willing and able to take? What if you buy shares and the market value then declines? How much loss should you accept before bailing out of a losing position—or, if you keep the stock, how long will it take to recover? These troubling questions plague everyone in the market.

With contingent purchase strategies, you make a relatively small dollar-value trade. If the stock moves up in the direction you expect, your option trade will be profitable. If the stock does not move as you expect, your loss is quite limited, especially compared to the alternative of buying shares. But this typical long position—buying calls for most people—is not the only strategy available to you. There are several others as well. These include the basic purchase of calls or sale of puts; spreads combining covered calls and uncovered puts; and straddles.

▪ Basic Contingent Purchase: Long Call or Short Put

The most basic of all contingent purchase strategies is the purchase of a call. Most option traders do not think of this trade as a true contingent purchase, but rather as a speculative play. The idea is that you buy the call, it increases in value when the stock price rises, and you sell at a profit. The problem with this assumption is that (1) stock prices do not always rise before expiration of the call, and (2) even when those prices do rise, you need to overcome the time value premium and experience *enough* growth to experience a profit. These are the reasons that 75 percent of all options expire worthless.

The long call becomes a contingent purchase in one of two circumstances. The first is the *automatic exercise* of the call. This occurs when the call is in the money on the day of expiration and you take no action. Your call may be exercised, so that you acquire 100 shares for each call owned, at the strike price. Most speculators close their long call positions before this occurs to avoid automatic exercise. The second circumstance creating contingent purchase comes into existence when you buy calls to lock in a price today, with the intention of buying shares before expiration.

In that second condition, contingent purchase is quite different from the other reasons you might buy calls. These include taking advantage of large price declines that you believe will rebound, and for some people, providing cover for short stock positions. When you buy calls to lock in the strike price as part of a contingent purchase strategy, the concept is fairly straightforward. You are willing to pay the premium today in exchange for the right to buy 100 shares of stock before expiration, *if and when* you decide to exercise the calls.

It makes sense to use this strategy for calls with strike prices extending out a few months, containing relatively little time value, and close to the desired strike price. Can such ideal calls be found? It is possible in some situations. There was a discussion in Chapter 3 concerning Citigroup. Table 3-1 listed a series of calls based on the stock price as of April 5, 2007. On that day, Citigroup was worth $51.57 per share. Two options were especially interesting in terms of contingent purchase. The April 50 calls were selling at 1.95 and the September 50 calls were at 3.50. The April 50 had only 0.38 time value and 1.57 intrinsic value. The call had 15 days to go until expiration. The September 50 call contained 1.93 time value and 1.57 intrinsic. For only $193, investors could purchase an in-the-money call with five months to go before expiration.

If you had been tracking Citigroup in April 2007 and wanted to buy shares at $50, these calls would probably have gotten your attention, notably the September 50. If you did not have the funds available, or if you were concerned about the possibility of a short-term price decline, you could buy a September 50 call for $350 and wait out the market.

Another variation of the same approach is selling puts. When you buy calls, you pay money and create a debit in your account; when you sell puts, you do the opposite. You create a credit in your account, placing you at a much greater advantage. If the short put expires worthless, you keep the money. If it is exercised, you have 100 shares put to you at the strike price (and your basis is the strike price minus the premium you received when you sold the put). This strategy makes sense when you believe the strike price is a fair price for the stock and when you are willing to accept exercise.

EXAMPLE

Referring again to the situation with Citigroup (in Table 3-1), instead of buying a September 50 call, you could sell a September 50 put. This put was worth 1.80 on April 5, 2007. So instead of paying $350, you would receive $180, a difference between the two strategies of $530. If the put were exercised, you would buy 100 shares of Citigroup at $50 per share and your basis would be $48.20 ($50 per share less 1.80 for the put). If the stock were between $48.20 and $50 per share at the time the put was exercised, your basis would be higher than your net cost. If the stock's price were below that level, you would have a paper loss.

Two things to remember about the paper loss: First, the strategy is based on an assumption that you consider $50 per share a good price for the stock, even if it falls below your net cost of $48.20 temporarily. Second, you can employ a recovery strategy involving the sale of a covered call. For example, if your paper loss was $2 per share and you could sell a 50 call for 3, you would eliminate the paper loss entirely and have $100 left over (before trading costs). If the covered call were exercised at 50, you would gain a profit in the stock of $180 ($50 less $48.20 net basis).

Using long calls and short puts as a form of contingent purchase makes sense in many circumstances and can help you to plan out your portfolio many months in advance. So many stockholders look back and beat themselves up because they didn't buy stock several months before, when the price was lower. With long calls and short puts, you can position yourself and your portfolio to plan ahead and create profits while doing away with the remorse of hindsight.

The Flip Side: Covered Calls for Contingent Sale

More advanced contingent purchase strategies are explained later in this chapter. First, though, it is important to talk about covered calls with an eye to the strategy of contingent sale of stock you currently own.

Most investors view covered calls as a low-risk method for improving current income from a portfolio with no added market risk. In fact, double-digit returns are not only possible—with properly selected covered calls, high returns are inevitable. So on the surface and without considering anything beyond current income, covered call writing is a smart, conservative, and profitable strategy. But there is more.

You can also use covered calls as part of a contingent sale strategy. Many investors do not consider this possibility; they believe that you either hold stock or you sell it, with no room for anything in between. But when you sell a covered call against 100 shares of stock, you can employ that method as a form of contingent sale. This action creates exercise at a price you desire, while also providing additional income from the short call.

The contingent sale strategy makes sense in several situations. Here are some of them:

* *You want to sell the stock because the fundamentals have changed.* Nothing remains the same forever. When you buy a company's stock based on strong fundamentals, you want the situation to remain strong, but that does not always happen. Once you realize this, it is time to sell. That can be done with a straight-out sale of the stock or through writing an in-the-money covered call. The latter creates additional premium income for you. However, be aware of the tax rules regarding writing deep in-the-money covered calls. (Chapter 8 explains the limitations and potential consequences.)

* *You would take profits now if the covered call were exercised, or you would be equally satisfied to keep the stock if the call's value falls.* In some situations, you are ambivalent about stock you own and would be willing to accept exercise. At the same time, you do not have a sense of urgency about dumping shares. This is the perfect situation for writing a covered call as a contingent sale decision.

- *You are operating the portfolio when taxes are not an issue.* As Chapter 8 explains in more detail, if you write deep in-the-money covered calls, you will lose long-term status for your stock. So if you have owned stock for many years and have considerable profit in the position, writing calls with the intention of creating certain exercise might make sense, as long as you know the tax consequences. There are two situations in which the loss of long-term capital gains status does not matter. The first is when you are managing a portfolio within a qualified retirement plan such as an IRA. Because all profits are deferred and eventually treated as ordinary income, you are not concerned with the elimination of long-term rates. The second situation is when you have a substantial carryover loss. You are allowed to deduct only $3,000 per year in net losses, so a large loss is going to take many years to absorb. Because of this, the elimination of long-term capital gains rates is not of immediate concern. You would rather absorb the carryover loss than continue carrying it for many years. In fact, in this situation, the contingent sales strategy is wise for two reasons. First, you can absorb the capital gains within the carryover loss. Second, you do not have to be concerned with realized capital gains and option premium income because the carryover loss shelters those current-year profits.

Most covered call writers view the strategy as a cash generator. The idea is to gain the premium income and repeat the strategy indefinitely. If and when exercise becomes likely, the position can be rolled forward and up, delaying expiration but avoiding having stock called away. The contingent sale, like the various contingent purchase strategies, moves this point of view into a broader venue, one in which portfolio management (including contingent purchase and sale) are structured to also generate income.

You can continue to use options for both points of view, as speculative or cash-generating devices *and* for portfolio management, either to purchase or sell shares. In spite of the commonly held belief that you cannot have it both ways, you can, by deferring the purchase of stock while locking in a contingent price, and generating income through covered calls in anticipation of exercise.

One argument against using covered calls for contingent sales involves decisive action. It is often true that once you decide that it is time to sell stock, you should execute the sell and not delay the decision. In fact, if the fundamentals have weakened, it could be dangerous to wait. Even with the covered call available to you, it might just make sense to sell the stock and invest in companies better suited to your goals.

The decision is a personal one. No formula makes it absolutely right or wrong to use covered calls in a particular case or involving a specific company. The point of view that covered calls work as a form of contingent sale of stock is one of many strategies worth considering. In managing your portfolio, this gives you a greater range of choices than simply limiting yourself to long stock positions and occasional option speculation.

The Combined Strategy: Covered Call and Naked Put Spread

One of the most intriguing strategies actually combines two offsetting elements: a contingent sale (covered call) and a contingent purchase (uncovered, or naked, put). By forming a spread with these two short positions, you create current income and also create a position in which it would be difficult to lose money.

You will recall that spreads consist of options with different strike prices, different expiration dates, or both. A spread may consist of long or short options and may include calls or puts or a combination of both. The contingent purchase strategy that follows is based on the simultaneous sale of a covered call and an uncovered put. A requisite for this position is ownership of 100 shares for each call sold, because this is a conservative strategy. Thus, if you were to write uncovered calls, that would contradict the requirement that a double-digit return is possible without high risk.

Let's look at an example. Consider the options available on IBM as of April 16, 2007. At the close that day, the stock was worth $96.18 per share and options were priced as shown in Table 6-1. The spread for IBM is going to involve two short positions, a covered call and an uncovered put. Before we get into the details, though, you need to be aware of when this strategy is appropriate:

- *You are willing to accept exercise on either side.* When you enter a short spread, you create two option posi-

TABLE 6-1. CALLS AND PUTS FOR IBM.

IBM, April 16, 2007 (closed at $96.18 per share)

Calls		premium	Puts		premium
MAY	95	2.85	MAY	95	1.60
	100	0.70		100	4.50
JUL	95	4.50	JUL	95	2.40
	100	2.00		100	5.20
OCT	95	6.10	OCT	95	3.50
	100	3.60		100	6.20
JAN (08)	95	7.83	JAN (08)	95	4.50
	100	5.10		100	6.90

tions, and either or both can be exercised. For example, you may pick a call above current stock price and a put below; sell both; and collect the premium, such as selling a July 100 call and a May 95 put. (An uncovered call would involve substantial risk, so it is not considered in this example.) Because you own stock, the short call is covered. The short spread makes sense only if you will be happy to accept exercise of either option, or of both options. (If both options are exercised, you end up with the same position you have before entering the spread, after you have 100 shares called away and another 100 put to you. The only variation arises from the net differences between strike prices, adjusted by the total premium you receive.)

- *If the short put is exercised, you are willing to acquire shares at the strike price.* If the put is exercised, you will be required to buy another 100 shares at the strike price. If exercise does occur, the market value of the 100 shares will be lower than the strike price you pay. You need to be able to accept this risk, based on your current belief that the put's strike price is a reasonable price for shares.

- *If the short call is exercised, you are willing to have your shares called away.* The spread also involves a covered call. You need to be willing to give up your 100 shares of stock at the strike price in order for the short spread to make sense.

- *There is enough premium income from the spread to justify opening the position.* Whenever you put yourself at risk with short options, you need to analyze the premium income to make sure it is worthwhile. The dollar amount and percentage of annualized return have to be rewarding enough, or the position will not make sense.

- *You understand the transaction completely and have analyzed all possible outcomes.* Most option surprises come up because a trader did not understand the full scope of risks involved. It is easy to focus on the profit potential without also realizing that there could be a loss. Any option transaction should be completely understood in advance.

Referring to Table 6-1, you could enter a short spread in a number of ways. First, consider a spread in which both sides are out of the money. This means that no exercise will occur unless the stock moves above the call's strike or below the put's strike. With the IBM stock at $96.18 at the close of the sample date, you would want to look at calls above that level and at puts below that level. For example, you may write a July 100 call worth 2.00 and a May 95 put valued at 1.60. The put expires in one month, the call in three months. Your total premium income would be $360, which is a 3.7 percent return. Annualized, the put, with only one month until expiration, yields 44.4 percent (3.7% x 12 months = 44.4); the call, with three months until expiration, provides a yield of 2.1 percent, or an annualized yield of 8.4 percent (2.1% ÷ 3 x 12 = 8.4%). Together, the call and put produce a total annualized yield of 52.8 percent. (It is important to remember, however, that calculations of annualized yield should be used for comparisons only, and not to develop a realistic expectation of yields you expect to realize consistently on your portfolio.)

One way to study the risk and potential income in this position is by treating the 3.60 option premium as a "safety zone" above the call's strike and below the put's. Figure 6-1 illustrates this concept.

The advantage to this spread is that the short put expires earlier than the short covered call. This means that

FIGURE 6-1. IBM SHORT SPREAD.

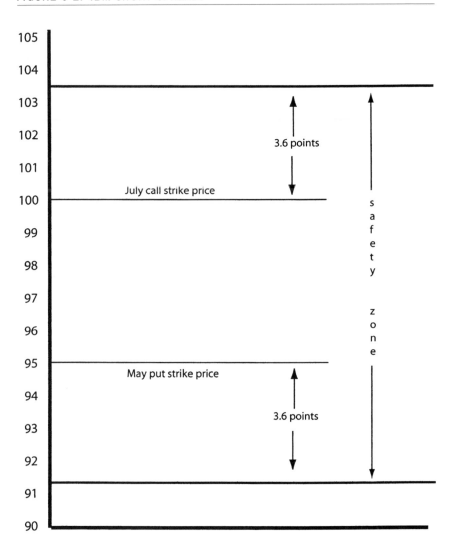

you would be able to replace the expired May put with a June or July short put upon expiration, further increasing current income. But without even considering that possibility, the 3.60 premium income from the spread creates a "safety zone" between the prices of $91.40 (95 put strike less 3.60) and $103.60 (100 call strike plus 3.60). If the stock's price remains within this zone, extending 12.2

points, the entire position will be profitable. While either option may be exercised, you can roll forward and up (for the call) or forward and down (for the put) to avoid exercise. If the stock's price moves above or below the defined safety zone, a different outcome occurs. Your 100 shares would be called away above $100 per share, and above the safety zone you would lose the potential profit if you had not written a call. If the stock moves below $95, the put will be exercised. Within the safety zone, exercise does not produce a loss; but if the stock is valued below $91.40, then you have a net loss from the spread. (That loss exists only on paper, however, and you can recover by writing later covered calls or repeating the spread position.)

Those short-term short positions produce double-digit returns on an annualized basis, which is quite satisfying for most people. However, you can produce even higher yields by writing options farther out until expiration. For example—referring again to Table 6-1—writing a January (2008) 100 call at 5.10 and an October 95 put at 3.50 yields a total of $860. The call's yield is 5.3 percent or, annualized, 7.1 percent (5.3% ÷ 9 months x 12 months). The put's return is 3.6 percent or, annualized, 7.2 percent (3.6% ÷ 6 x 12). The overall return in this case represents 14.3 percent. Note that while the annualized yield is substantially lower than in the shorter-term examples, the dollar amount you receive is much higher. This disparity results from the important differences in the time involved. Furthermore, these comparisons assume that all option positions would be left open all the way until expiration. In practical terms, it is far more likely that these short positions would be closed once time value declines, or rolled forward and replaced.

Because the dollar amounts are so much greater, the "safety zone" for this spread would be 8.6 points above the 100 call strike, and 8.6 points below the put's 95 strike price. That creates a safety zone of 22.2 points (from

$86.40 up to $108.60 per share). The short spread can also be written more aggressively, using in-the-money positions. For example, you could write May 95 calls worth 2.85 and May 100 puts for 4.50, receiving a total of $735. This is a one-month yield of 7.6 percent, annualized 91.2 percent—again, not a reliable measurement of what you could expect to earn consistently on your portfolio but valuable as a comparative test. One reason the one-month yield is so high is that both options are in the money. Chances are high that one or both of these options would be exercised, which raises another twist on the in-the-money short spread strategy. If the stock value remains in between the strike prices until expiration, both options would be exercised. That means that you buy 100 shares at the $100 put strike and sell your current holdings of 100 shares at $95 per share. That represents a net loss in the difference between strike prices of $500—but you received $735. So the "worst-case" outcome in this spread would be a $235 profit. You started out with 100 shares of stock and end up with 100 shares:

Beginning position	100 shares held
100 shares put to you	+100
100 shares called away	−100
Ending position	100 shares held

The degree of profit, in terms of dollar as well as percentages, is going to vary between stocks.

EXAMPLE

In Table 6-2, a series of calls and puts are listed for Microsoft as of the closing of April 16, 2007. At that time, Microsoft was worth $28.73 per share. (Dollar values of options were much lower than for the higher-priced IBM options shown in Table 6-1, and percentage returns vary

TABLE 6-2. CALLS AND PUTS FOR MICROSOFT.

Microsoft, April 16, 2007 (closed at $28.73 per share)

Calls		premium	Puts		premium
MAY	27.50	1.56	MAY	27.50	0.29
	30	0.26		30	1.52
JUL	27.50	1.97	JUL	27.50	0.54
	30	0.63		30	1.69
OCT	27.50	2.59	OCT	27.50	0.88
	30	1.15		30	2.00
JAN (08)	27.50	3.10	JAN (08)	27.50	1.18
	30	1.66		30	2.26

as well.) If you were to write a short spread selling an October 30 call for 1.15 and an October 27.50 put for 0.88, you would receive only $203. The return would be 7.1 percent, or annualized 14.2 percent, for these six-month positions. Considering that these positions contain the same exercise risks as other short spreads, you may question whether the six-month exposure would be worthwhile for only $203.

EXAMPLE

Table 6-3 shows a range of call and put values for Bank of America. On April 16, 2007, the stock closed at $51.23 per share. A short spread could involve a November 52.50 call for 1.15 and an August 52.50 put for 1.69. The total premium would be $284. Over the seven-month period, that is a return of 5.5 percent, or annualized 9.4 percent. So a critical question would be: Do you want to be at risk for seven months for a 9.4 percent return and only $284?

Based on the three examples presented in the preceding pages—IBM, Microsoft, and Bank of America—the

TABLE 6-3. CALLS AND PUTS FOR BANK OF AMERICA.

Bank of America, April 16, 2007 (closed at $51.23 per share)

Calls		premium	Puts		premium
MAY	50	1.56	MAY	50	0.29
	52.50	0.26		52.50	1.52
AUG	50	1.97	AUG	50	0.54
	52.50	0.63		52.50	1.69
NOV	50	2.59	NOV	50	0.88
	52.50	1.15		52.50	2.00
JAN (08)	50	3.10	JAN (08)	50	1.18
	52.50	1.66		52.50	2.26

dollar values and returns for IBM were far greater than for Microsoft or Bank of America. Short spreads work for all three. However, the overall returns—especially for out-of-the-money short spreads—were more favorable for IBM at that time. This does not mean it will always be the case. As volatility levels change for a company, and when you compare short-term versus long-term options, you soon realize that the outcome of a short spread is going to depend on values at the moment and not in conformity with an assumed standard.

Contingent Purchase Straddles

You can also write contingent purchase straddles. Because one side of the transaction involves a contingent purchase (the put) and the other a contingent sale (the call), this strategy could lead to exercise on both sides. If the stock remained near the strike price at expiration, it is conceivable that you could have both a sale and a purchase, ending up where you began, having your stock called away *and* put to you—with the option premium clear profit.

A straddle involves the trading of options with identical strike and expiration. So a short straddle—a call and a put—should consist of a covered call and an uncovered put. As with the spread strategy, you can use uncovered calls, but that involves far greater risks. The contingent purchase straddle strategy is ideal because it is low-risk, given the covered call.

As with all short option strategies, you have to be willing to accept exercise of either or both sides of the transaction. This means that your stock could be called away *or* that you could have another 100 shares put to you at the strike price. As long as you think the strike price is reasonable, and you are also confident that you would be able to recover a paper loss after exercise, the strategy is a sound one.

EXAMPLE

Referring again to Table 6-1, you could write a short straddle on IBM. The beginning assumption is that you own 100 shares of stock, in order to ensure that the short call is covered. The stock closed on the example day at $96.18 per share. The closest strike is 95. The May 95 call closed at 2.85 and the May 95 put at 1.60. If you sell these two options, you receive $445. With only one month of exposure to the short position, the return is 4.6 percent, or annualized 55.2 percent—not a bad return, assuming you are comfortable with the likelihood of exercise.

The strategy creates a safety zone of 9 points, 4.5 above and 4.5 below strike. This is shown in Figure 6-2. This means that even in the event of exercise, as long as the stock closes between $90.55 and $99.45 per share, the straddle will be profitable (even with exercise on either side). If the stock closes above that level, the strategy remains profitable, but you lose the potential profits you

FIGURE 6-2. IBM SHORT STRADDLE.

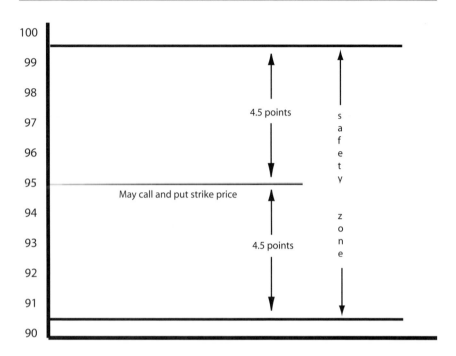

would have gained if you had not written the covered call. If the stock ends up below $90.55 and the put is exercised, you will have a paper loss. This can be recovered if you write subsequent covered calls on the 200 shares you would then own or if you develop another contingent purchase straddle or spread.

The straddle is more restrictive than the spread. With a spread, you can set the trade up so that both sides are out of the money, and then roll forward to avoid exercise. You can also roll out of the straddle positions, depending on the direction of the stock price movement, but exercise is more likely because one side is always in the money. You can also increase premium income by allowing the straddle to remain open for a longer period.

EXAMPLE

Referring to Table 6-1, if you are willing to go out three months, you could write an IBM July 95 call for 4.50 and a 95 put for 2.40, receiving a total of $690. This provides you with a broader safety zone. At the same time, you can still roll out of exercise on either side. When you do that, you convert the straddle into a spread. If the out-of-the-money side of the transaction loses enough value, it can be closed at a profit. That creates a short option position. If you close the put, you end up with a covered call; if you close the short call, you end up with an uncovered put.

Income potential for the same strategy described in the above example using Microsoft would not be as profitable. The dollar values are not as high, because Microsoft was selling at less than one-third of IBM's share price, and Microsoft was also less volatile in 2007. For example, referring to Table 6-2, you could set up a short straddle using May 27.50 calls for 1.56 and May 27.50 puts at 0.29. You would receive a total of $185, or 6.4 percent (annualized 76.8 percent). But even with the higher comparative annualized yield, is this position worth the exposure? Considering that the put premium is only $29, why risk it? You would improve the position by making it a spread or simply writing a covered call and not involving the put side.

Table 6-3 summarized option values for Bank of America. The same argument applies here: Put premium values are quite low at the 50 strike, and call premium values are low at the 52.50 strike. For both Microsoft and Bank of America in the reported positions of stock price and options, the straddle would not be the best possible strategy (especially compared to spreads or covered calls). The situation could easily change if the prices moved closer to a strike in either direction.

■ Varying the Balance of the Spread or Straddle

There is no limit to the variation you can apply to spreads and straddles. The examples in this chapter assume ownership of 100 shares and going short on one call and one put, but you can expand the strategy using multiple contracts as well.

You are limited by margin requirements in how many uncovered puts you can write. As a usual requirement, you have to keep at least one half of a short put's strike price on deposit. For example, if the strike is 50, you need to maintain a $2,500 balance in your margin account, so you could not simply write hundreds of short puts. However, you can vary the balance. For example, if you own 1,000 shares of stock, you can write up to ten covered calls. At the same time, you do not have to write ten short puts. You can create a number of spreads and straddles and create a weighted situation in which you have a greater number of covered calls than uncovered puts.

EXAMPLE

The values reflected in Table 6-1 for IBM show how this can be achieved. You can also spread your positions over a period of time. If you decided to write ten covered calls and four uncovered puts on IBM, you could employ any number of combinations. For example:

	Premium	Return	Annualized
2 May 95 calls @ 2.85	$ 570	3.0	36.0%
2 July 100 calls @ 2.00	400	2.1	8.4
3 October 100 calls @ 3.60	1,080	3.7	7.4
3 January (2008) 100 calls @ 5.10	1,530	5.3	7.1
4 January (2008) 95 puts @ 4.50	1,800	4.7	6.3
total	$5,380		65.2%

The annualization, as always, is useful only for comparisons and not to set a likely outcome for your portfolio. The point to remember in this example is that writing multiple-contracts spreads and straddles provides a lot of flexibility. Any of these short positions can be rolled forward and up (for calls) or down (for puts) to avoid exercise, further increasing option premium income and, if exercise does occur, a more favorable outcome.

Avoiding exercise should be done in such a way that a net credit is created. This is not difficult, although it does require extending the period of exposure. For example, the values shown in Table 6-1 can apply to any situation and any price level. You have to assume that if the stock's price rises, call values will also rise and put values will fall—and vice versa. So if you had sold a May 95 covered call and you anticipated that it would be exercised within the next month, you could buy to close at 2.85 and replace it with an October 100, which is worth 3.60. You gain $75 in credit for this forward roll, *and* you also pick up 5 points in strike price. This means that if the call is eventually exercised, that will occur at $100 per share instead of $95.

The same kind of rolling can be used with puts. For example, continuing with Table 6–1, if you had sold a May 100 put worth 4.50, you could buy it to close and replace it with a January (2008) 95, worth 4.50. You exchange puts valued the same, but you reduce the exercise price by 5 points. You would be charged transaction fees for the purchase and the sale of the two put contracts—but if and when the put is exercised, you would be required to pay $500 less for the stock. Another alternative would be to buy the May 100 put and sell a later 100 put, creating a credit but leaving the strike at the same level.

In a spread or straddle, you would roll only one side at

a time. For example, if you had written a short straddle and the stock's price rose, you would roll the short call forward and up to avoid exercise. In that situation, the short put would be out of the money, so it could be left intact. However, if the stock later began declining in value, you could roll the short put forward and down, avoiding exercise. In this example, you extend the safety zone of the position, gaining additional income and creating higher call strike and lower put strike. In other words, spreads and straddles are not rigid or set; they can be modified any number of times to avoid exercise.

Spreads and straddles are effective tools for expanding your current portfolio, within a contingent purchase plan. You can simply sell uncovered puts, gain premium income, and accept exercise as one approach. Or you can employ the more profitable spread and straddle ideas to gain a powerful advantage in terms of stock prices and current income.

Many investors—even those restricting their activity to long-term value investments—recognize the short-term speculative opportunities in the market. Without violating your long-term goals and risk tolerance levels, you can use options to profit from short-term price overreaction. The common techniques used for day trading and swing trading restrict your trading simply because of limited supplies of cash and margin account levels. However, with options you can control 100 shares of stock and effectively day and swing trade for little risk. This is one situation in which the use of soon-to-expire options with little or no time value can be used most effectively, even on the long side. This is the topic of Chapter 7.

OPTIONS FOR
SHORT-TERM PROFITS

"Civilization and profits go hand in hand."
—Calvin Coolidge, November 27, 1920

THE TYPICAL DISTINCTION between long-term investing and outright speculation is quite broad, often with little room in between. The tendency is to group people into those favoring one extreme or the other. Long-term investors, also called *value investors,* tend to be quite conservative and risk-adverse. On the other hand, speculators tend to be reckless and willing to put their capital at risk in pursuit of exceptional profits.

There is room for a balance in most portfolios. For example, you already know that it is possible to use options to speculate on short-term price aberrations, or even to write short spreads and straddles as part of a low-risk contingent purchase plan. These strategies are usually classified as very high-risk. Even so, as Chapter 6 demonstrated, the risk has to be qualified. For example, as long as the short call side of a combination is a covered call, the only question remaining is whether you are willing to risk having a short put exercised. Given the high return possible from a well-designed contingent strategy, it is clear that even the most conservative risk profile can benefit from option strategies, and this is true in many forms.

There is more to this distinction. It is also possible for you to continue maintaining a highly conservative portfolio *and* still benefit from short-term price movement. As long as you do not compromise your risk tolerance levels or place capital at risk that you cannot afford to lose, you can devise many strategies aimed at creating short-term profit potential apart from your permanent portfolio. This involves a series of timing trades commonly called a *day trading* strategy.

This term refers not only to the extremely short-term nature of the trades in and out of positions but also to the common practice of opening and closing positions within a single day. Historically, day traders have used stocks as well as options, opening and closing trades in high volume, and often leveraging tremendous profits (and losses) with little capital at risk.

This is where problems have arisen. The margin requirements imposed on trading accounts are well known, but they apply to end-of-day balances. For example, if you buy stock on margin, you are required to have at least 50 percent of the current value kept in your account. However, if you move in and out of stock or option positions and close them out by the end of the day, you escape the margin requirement altogether. For this reason, the Securities and Exchange Commission (SEC) devised the pattern day trading rule (see Chapter 4). This rule states that if you make four or more trades within five consecutive trading days, you are classified as a pattern day trader. You are then required to keep at least $25,000 in your account. If you do not maintain this minimum balance, you are banned from any further trades in the stock or its options until you meet the cash requirement.

This rule shut down many of the more abusive day trading practices. Today, only those traders who maintain a high enough balance are allowed to transact high-volume trades. However, the rule also created a new type of short-term strategy, known as *swing trading*. This is defined as a series of trades opened and closed within three to five consecutive trading days (there may be more days involved, but the three- to five-day time frame is most common).

This chapter shows how swing trading can be a good fit even for the most conservative portfolio, and how you can use options as part of a swing trading strategy. Options allow you to diversify your swing trading exposure with high leverage and for relatively low risk. Compared to swing trading using shares of stock, using options provides you with greater flexibility and helps you to avoid the big problem with swing trading: the need to go short on half of all trades. With options, you can play the short side of a trade using long puts instead of shorting stock. This makes options ideal for swing trading, and as long as you make a distinction between your long-term portfolio goals and the short-term swing trading activity, you can employ both without violating your risk tolerance level.

The Contrarian Approach

When you pick stocks, you probably use several fundamental indicators to narrow down your list. These may include dividend rate, revenue and earnings, debt ratio, current ratio, P/E ratio, and other value-based tests. If you are a value investor, you then seek companies whose stock is available at a bargain price.

This is a sensible method for choosing stocks, and if you have done the job properly, you can be confident that the long-term growth of your portfolio is a likely outcome. Within the framework of a value investing approach, you are supposed to ignore the chaotic and often illogical short-term trend. Most fundamental investors understand that short-term price movement is not dependable information for trend analysis. Even technicians know this and agree. Proponents of the Dow Theory and other technical schools of thought generally acknowledge that day-to-day price movement involves too many variables to be useful for making long-term decisions.

However, if you also subscribe to the contrarian point of view, you recognize that short-term price movement also represents an opportunity. Most investors (including institutional investors like mutual funds, insurance companies, and pension plans) are reactive. They see a price rise and they buy; they see the price fall and they sell. The majority of investors are wrong more often than they are right. This observation forms the basis of the *contrarian approach* to investing.

As a contrarian, you are supposed to do the opposite of what most people are doing. So when a stock's price rises suddenly and unexpectedly, and you see that everyone is buying, you resist the temptation. You sell at the top, while most other people are buying. When you see a stock's share price plummet, you observe that most investors are scared and they sell their stock to cut their losses. But as a contrarian, you tend to keep your head and recognize a buying opportunity.

How do these contrarian rules fit with your long-term portfolio? The general rule of thumb is that you buy strongly managed, competitive companies at bargain prices and then ignore the market until the situation changes. Most portfolio management theories shun the more speculative concept of trading every day and moving in and out of positions. However, with options, you can play those short-term price movements and use a stock's volatility to create profits. Long-term investors do not want a high degree of volatility in their portfolios; they prefer slow, steady growth. There are conditions, though, in which even the safest stocks become temporarily volatile. In those times, you can use swing trading techniques to move against the market. As a contrarian, you can profit by buying into opportunities, when the price is exceptionally low *and* when the price is unrealistically high.

Swing trading is one of those strategic ideas that looks and sounds good. But when you realize that you need a lot of cash to maximize the strategy, it does not seem practical. In addition, if you use stock to swing trade, half of your trades involve going short, and that is a high-risk strategy. Swing trading makes no sense for most people because of these severe limitations. Options remove all of the risk and monetary restrictions, meaning that using long calls and puts enables you to control a lot of stock for very little money, and for a limited amount of risk.

Emotions That Rule the Market

Swing trading is based on a simple premise: The market is ruled by emotions and not by science. One might assume the opposite. After all, the most analytical fundamental investor develops a series of sensible reasons to buy a stock. The rationale is based on the numbers. The *concept* is sound. Even so, you have probably bought stock for all of the right reasons only to see its price fall as soon as your trade goes in. Why does this happen?

Put aside all of the logic for a moment. It is important to understand that for picking long-term investments, the principles of value investing make a lot of sense. You need to be analytical to pick stocks intelligently. But when you look at how the market moves from one day to the next, you realize that analytical processes have absolutely nothing to do with the price of stock or with the point movement within a day.

EXAMPLE

A company's earnings beat estimates by three cents per share and, as a result, the stock's price jumps 3 percent in a single day. Is that an overreaction? Of course it is. In another case, a company is subject to a rumor. The SEC might be investigating the company's compensation policy, the CEO is about to be fired, or there are going to be lawsuits having to do with product liability. Even if these kinds of rumors are untrue, on the day they are going around, a stock's price could fall several points.

It all comes down to three emotions. The market is guided by these emotions, and day-to-day price changes are normally exaggerated based on actual facts. These emotions are:

1. *Fear.* When prices fall, it is difficult for investors to maintain a cool head, especially if panic is widespread. Without thinking clearly, people's tendency is to sell when prices fall, to avoid even deeper losses. For the contrarian, however, the time to get into a stock is when its price has fallen. If traders are going to react to overall market sentiment, it is quite difficult to adopt a contrarian point of view. This is why a highly disciplined and programmed approach to the timing of trades is such a valuable tool.

2. *Greed.* The same tendency works in reverse. When prices rise, more and more people buy stock. The higher the price moves, the more the tendency to want to get in on the profits. It makes no sense to overpay for stock; even so, the crowd mentality of the market brings people in at the worst possible time, when stocks are overpriced and due for a correction.

3. *Uncertainty.* At times, often after a big price movement, a stock's share price retreats into a narrow trading range. Prices do not rise or fall substantially, often for a period of several days. This narrow trading range often foreshadows a coming price movement, but it is impossible to tell which direction that will take. In periods of uncertainty, buyers and sellers settle down into a sort of "agreement" about the stock's current value. That changes soon enough, but for the astute contrarian, when the market is uncertain, it is not time to buy or sell but to remain on the sidelines and wait for the next short-term trend to present itself.

Because these emotions rule the market in the short term, there is a tendency among traders to buy high and sell low, instead of the more profitable rule to "buy low and sell high." If you observe the emotional roller coaster of the market, you notice that fear, greed, and uncertainty do indeed determine when and how traders move in and out of stocks. It is predictable.

This is the great observation that swing traders use to create short-term profits. You will notice that whenever a stock's price moves over a period of a few days in one direction, it tends to correct or reverse itself. Even if the overall trend is in the direction of strong movement, prices never move in one direction without pause. As prices rise, some traders take profits (which brings the price back down). As prices fall, other investors pick up bargains (which causes prices to rise). This seemingly orderly process is anything but orderly, because those three emotions distort price movement, exaggerating both the initial movement *and* the correction. The supply and demand that is always present in the market is not efficient or predictable. What is predictable is that all price movements are going to exceed the sensible indicators underlying the movement itself, and those same prices will correct in an equal overreaction. The market moves like a teenager learning to drive a stick shift—in a series of surges and jarring stops.

Day Trading Techniques

Anyone trading in a very short time horizon—such as within a single day—is generally assumed to be a speculator, willing to take high risks. This is not always true. Exposure in a position defines the risk profile to strategies, and not the time involved.

A day trader is anyone who moves in and out of positions rapidly, usually opening and closing a trade within one day. For such quick turnover in trades, options may be entirely inappropriate because small changes in the stock are not always reflected in option valuation, even when options are in the money. Movement of the option premium is going to be less responsive when time and extrinsic value remains; and the more time and extrinsic value, the more tendency for the option to underreact to price movement.

You see this tendency in all stocks and options. For example, an option in the money with three months to go until expiration will not track the stock precisely. Changes in both time value and extrinsic value create a situation in which the option premium changes are often quite different from changes in the stock. While intrinsic value tracks stock prices point for point in the money, the overall premium does not always reflect that change.

Consider three examples based on prices about 90 minutes before the close of April 20, 2007, a day selected because it was option expiration day, so a lot of activity in options about to expire is to be expected.

EXAMPLE #1

Kroger was at $30.11 per share, up 0.03 at that point, but the April 25 calls were at 5.20, up 0.20. Those options are set to expire after the trading day, but what is the explanation for the difference between the stock rise of three cents and the option rise of 20 cents? It is the pending expiration itself that accounts for the higher rise in extrinsic value (there was virtually no time value remaining at this point). Intrinsic value based on stock price of $30.11 was 5.11 and the total premium was 5.20 (and had previously been 5.00).

EXAMPLE #2

If you look at a stock with an option one month to expiration and just out of the money, you have a much different picture, but an even more glaring disparity. On the same day, Merck was at $51.43, up 1.28 per share. However, the May 52.50 calls were at 0.65, up 0.30. The stock rose 1.28, and the option was nearly a full point behind. This is because the option is still out of the money; there is no intrinsic value. The entire change in this premium is extrinsic in nature, but the premium did not pace the stock.

EXAMPLE #3

Yet another example for the same day was Citigroup, which was at $53.17, up 0.08. However, the June 55 calls were *down* 0.08, a difference of 16 cents and movement in the opposite direction. The call was out of the money with two months to go, so you would have to assume that this small decline in the face of a modest stock price rise is a combination of declining time value and extrinsic value.

These examples show why day trading can be very elusive. If a day trader uses options and bases timing on the normal fundamentals of stock movement combined with expected volatility in options, the plan can easily go wrong—as these examples demonstrate. The short-term movement of option premium, especially on high-volume days *and* the last trading days before option expiration, are highly unpredictable.

Day trading using stocks can be expensive and equally risky when compared to options. If a day trader is playing short-term price swings within a single day, the whole matter becomes very speculative. Day trading for most investors is not going to be appropriate. The strategy was popular a few years ago based on well-publicized cases of traders making extraordinary profits with little or no cash in their accounts. Going in and out of a trade got around the margin requirements, which are based on balances as of the end of the trading day. Since a day trader's balances are zero, there was no margin requirement. The pattern day trading rule curtailed a large segment of the day trading market; the rest fell off in periods of down markets. Day traders were often attracted to profit potential in up markets, using long stocks to make profits, so when prices fell, the plan failed. Today, day trading is widely recognized as high-risk. However, swing trading is a vastly different strategy and not nearly as risky as day trading. This is so because swing traders rely on price patterns developing over three to five days, and with decisions timed to specific price patterns.

Swing Trading as an Alternative

Swing trading often makes a lot of sense even when day trading does not, if only because the techniques that swing traders use are quite methodical and specific. Patterns taking three to five days to develop provide more certainty than the hour-to-hour changes in prices within a single day.

By definition, a swing trader moves in and out of positions over a three- to five-day time frame based on set-up pricing patterns. The set-up is a signal flagging the end of a short-term price movement and the pending reversal. The set-up tells the swing trader that when prices have been rising, the trend is going to turn and head downward. When prices have been moving downward, the set-up indicates the end of the decline and anticipates price movement on the way up.

These short-term trends are reflections of the fear (forcing prices down) and greed (forcing prices up) that dominate the market. When the third emotion, uncertainty, dominates, it is seen in a period of days with very little price change. This so-called "consolidation" is assumed to be a time when buyers and sellers are in momentary agreement about the price of stock. But it is more likely that the lack of price movement occurs because traders are on the sidelines waiting to see what is going to happen next. There is probably no time when both sides of a transaction are in complete agreement; buyers always want to pay less and sellers always want to receive more. Swing traders observe the price movement of stock as a reflection of unsettled short-term fear, greed, or uncertainty. That is the key to successful swing trading.

To visualize the specific price movements and set-ups, the easiest format for analysis is the candlestick chart. This is a type of charting system using a rectangular box with lines extending above and below. A white box indicates a day in which the closing price was higher than the opening price; a black box is a down day, in which the close was lower than the open. The top and bottom borders of the rectangle define the opening and closing prices. The lines extending above and below define the extent of the day's trading range. Candlestick types are summarized in Figure 7-1. The color of the candlestick tells you immediately which direction the stock moved; the body shows the breadth between open and close; and the shadows (lines above and below the rectangle) show you the extent of the day's trading range.

The swing trading strategy relies on identifying the set-up based on three- to five-day trends. An *uptrend* is a three- to five-day price movement in which each day's trading range is characterized by a series of progressively higher high prices, offset by a series of higher low prices. Each day's closing price is higher than its opening price, and the uptrend must continue for at least three days. A *downtrend* is a three- to five-day movement in which each day's trading is characterized by a series of progressively lower lows and lower highs. These patterns are illustrated in Figure 7-2, using the candlestick chart format.

This basic set-up for swing trading defines the trend itself. After a period of three or more days of continued trend in one direction, the swing trader looks for a *reversal signal*. That means the trend is ending and about to turn and move in the opposite direction. When you study can-

FIGURE 7-1. CANDLESTICK CHARTS.

up day

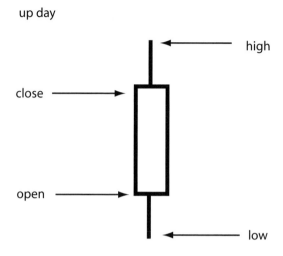

down day

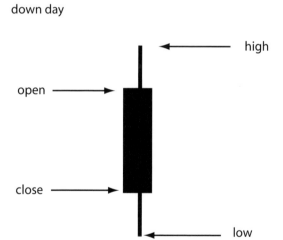

FIGURE 7-2. CANDLESTICK CHARTS SHOWING UPTRENDS AND DOWNTRENDS.

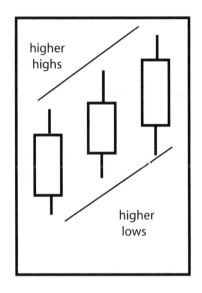

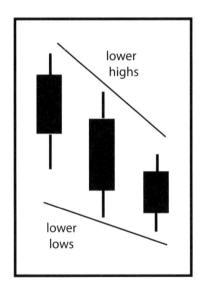

dlestick charts, you cannot always recognize a specific trend or set-up. A prudent swing trader enters into a swing trade only when the signals are present. At times, the trend will last longer than three days, so you may need to wait out the movement of price until a reversal signal appears.

EXAMPLE

General Electric displayed a very strong downtrend during the first two weeks of April 2007. After seven straight downtrend days, the pattern ended, as shown in Figure 7-3. The downtrend is clear in its shape and progression. Although the "rule" of lower lows and lower highs was not strictly followed, the trend is clear, and so is its end. Once an up

FIGURE 7-3. TRENDS FOR GENERAL ELECTRIC.

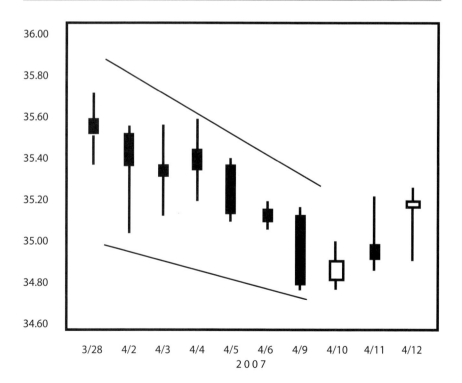

day occurs, it signals that the price direction is going to begin moving opposite the established trend.

The minimum three-day trend establishes the direction, but clearly, the trend can last much longer. The simplest form of reversal is the set-up of a day in which trading moves in the opposite direction. But two stronger set-up signals should be remembered as well. These are the *narrow-range day (NRD)* and exceptionally high volume. When the price pattern continues the existing trend but exhibits a combination of the NRD *and* very high volume, that is the strongest possible set-up signal for the end of the trend.

The NRD is easily spotted. It is a day where the distance between opening and closing prices is exceptionally small, as shown in Figure 7-4. Whether occurring at the end of an uptrend or a downtrend, the NRD warns you that the range of trading is small, meaning it is likely that the price direction is about to move in the opposite direction. If confirmed by surprisingly high volume, it is a very clear signal that a reversal is about to occur.

Using Options for Swing Trading

Swing trading makes sense as long as the set-up signals and trending patterns are present. It takes patience to wait for the ideal pattern to emerge, and like all systems, swing trading is not flawless. Perhaps its greatest flaw involves the problems when shares of stock are used as part of a swing trading strategy. Here are some of these problems:

• *Capital limits how much swing trading you can do at any one time.* You can only swing trade to the extent

FIGURE 7-4. NARROW-RANGE DAYS.

Uptrend

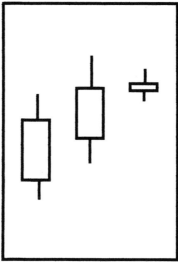

Downtrend

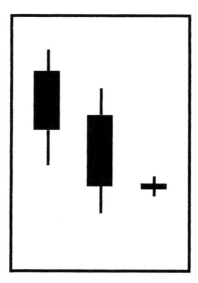

you have cash available. This means you have to pass some swing trading opportunities or use small increments of stock. For example, if you want to swing trade a stock worth $50 per share, a 100-share play requires $5,000. The number of stocks you can swing trade is limited accordingly, and the problem with buying and selling stock is that it cuts into your available capital. The more cash you use to swing trade, the smaller your long-term hold portfolio.

- *Using stock involves market risks.* When you buy and sell shares of stock, you expose yourself to a point-for-point risk in that stock. If the price moves in a direction opposite of one you anticipate, you lose one dollar per share per point. This is the same risk you face in your long-term portfolio, but because swing trading is designed as a quick in-and-out strategy, you may end up with a series of paper losses, unable to sell odd lot holdings without losing money.

- *To take advantage of the uptrend reversal, you have to sell short.* The greatest limitation to swing trading with stock is that to open a position at the top of a price trend, you need to sell short. Most people agree that short selling is a high-risk strategy. You also need to borrow the stock from your broker in order to sell and pay interest on the borrowed stock. For swing trading, shorting stock is awkward and risky.

All of these problems are solved by using options in a swing trading strategy:

- *You can swing trade many more issues with much less cash using options instead of stock.* When you use options, you can diversify into a much broader range of stocks, meaning you can also track some in upswings and others in downswings. Options control 100 shares of stock for a small fraction of the price, so leverage is another advantage to options in a swing trading strategy. For example, a $50 stock requires a $5,000 investment for 100 shares. But you can swing trade with single options for 10 percent or less of the cost of 100 shares. Thus, the same $5,000 can be used to play ten different stocks or to use multiples to augment swing trading profits.

- *While risk cannot be entirely avoided, using options is less risky than using stocks to swing trade.* Because you control 100 shares of stock with each option for much less money, the most you can lose is the entire long option value. This is a risk, of course, but compared to potential losses with shares of stock, the actual risk for options is much smaller.

- *With options, you can remain long on both sides of the transaction, enabling you to avoid the risk of short selling.* The big problem of needing to sell stock short is easily overcome with options. At the bottom of a downtrend, you buy calls; at the top of an uptrend, you sell those calls and buy puts in anticipation of the reversal pattern. By using long calls and puts instead of going long and short on stock, you reduce both cash requirements and risk levels.

Swing trading is also a valuable strategy when it comes to timing. When you buy options in most circumstances, you want to gain as much time as possible. You need time for the stock value to move in the money to make the option more valuable. But with swing trading, you intend to have positions open for only three to five days in most situations. So the short-term option—one expiring in one month, for example—is ideal for swing trading purposes.

Short-term options are perfect for another reason. If you pick options slightly in the money, there will be very little time value remaining because expiration will come up within a matter of a few weeks. With the majority of premium representing intrinsic value, the option is going to be far more likely to track movement of the stock's price. So if the stock moves 3 points further in the money, the option is likely to mimic that price movement or come very close to it. Because time value and extrinsic value will not be major factors, the option premium value is more reliable in tracking in-the-money values of the stock. Thus, with an in-the-money option, the potential profit in swing trading will be very close to the profit you would gain trading 100 shares of stock, at a far smaller cost.

For this strategy to work, it is essential to pick options immediately above strike (for calls) or below strike (for puts) to gain maximum advantage for minimum investment. If the options you use are out of the money, you will not get the same responsive price movement, so swing trading will not work. If you pick options farther in the money, you will have to pay much more to open positions, which is not necessary.

▪ Swing Trading with Options, Not Stocks

When you compare actual outcome with investment levels in mind, you realize that the return on options is far higher than for stocks, with lower risks involved.

EXAMPLE #1

Consider General Electric, which closed at $35.13 on April 20, 2007. The stock's price had been slipping all week from about $35.50 down to a low of $35. It appeared that the downtrend stalled on Friday, April 20; a swing trader might be looking for a short-term call slightly in the money. The April options last traded on April 20, so the next expiration was May. The stock was at $35.13, only 13 cents above the 35 strike. The GE May 35 call was worth 0.64.

EXAMPLE #2

Another example based on the same timing of option expiration is Harley-Davidson. The stock rose in the days before April 20, from $61 per share up to the April 20 close of $64.82. A swing trader would be interested in buying a put slightly in the money. Harley-Davidson was 18 cents below the 65 strike put. The May 65 put was worth 1.50.

These two examples demonstrate that for $64 in the first case and $150 in the second, you could enter a swing trade. To control the same 100 shares using stock, you would need to invest $6,482 (Harley) and $3,500 (General Electric). Assuming you would be able to double the option value ($150 for Harley and $64 for GE) within three to five days based on a short-term downtrend, the return is quite significant in options compared to stocks:

Harley-Davidson
Option investment = $150
Increased value = $300
Return = 100%

Stock investment = $6,482
Increased value = $6,632
Return = 2.3%

General Electric
Option investment = $64
Increased value = $128
Return = 100%

Stock investment = $3,513
Increased value = $3,577

Return = 1.8%

The return on stock in three to five days would not be bad; in fact, on an annualized basis, it would be very impressive. However, the exercise proves that using options is cheaper, allows you to use your capital for more broad swing trading activity, and contains much less risk.

The swing trading strategy with options can take one of two forms: a call and put strategy, and a call only strategy. The two examples above involving Harley-Davidson and General Electric demonstrate the call and put strategy, that you buy calls at the bottom of a downswing and that you buy puts at the top of the upswing. With the second strategy, involving only calls, at the bottom of a downswing, you buy calls, and at the top of the upswing, you sell calls. This is a sensible strategy, however, *only* if you also own the stock and the call is covered. So a typical series of trades involving two parts in either strategy would be:

Call and put strategy

- At the bottom of a downswing—buy a call

- At the top of an upswing—sell the long call and buy a put

- At the bottom of the next downswing—sell the put and buy a call

Call only strategy

- At the bottom of a downswing—buy a call

- At the top of an upswing—sell the long call and sell a covered call

- At the bottom of the next downswing—buy the covered call (to close) and buy a long call (to open)

The swing trading strategy works in conjunction with your long-term portfolio. It serves as a methodical tool for timing your purchase of options to play the short-term price swings. In previous chapters, the concept of speculating in both calls and puts to take profits or to gain price bargains was justified as a means of making those moves without disturbing the stocks in your portfolio. The tendency for many investors is to sell stocks to either take profits or cut losses; with options, you do not need to do either. Swing trading simply provides you with a powerful timing mechanism for those trades.

This is why swing trading is appropriate. It is not a method for mere speculation that would be inappropriate for the typical conservative investor or value investor. It is not just speculation. Consider the two typical scenarios:

1. You buy 100 shares of stock and within a short time, the price rises dramatically. Is this temporary? Should you take profits now? Should you wait to see if even more profit comes into the stock? Or should you follow the value investing rules and ignore short-term price movements?

2. You buy 100 shares of stock and the market goes through a severe correction of several 100 points. Your stock loses 15 percent of its value. Have you made a terrible mistake? Will the stock continue to decline? Should you sell now and cut your losses?

Both of these situations occur regularly in the market. Using options to take profits at the top or to get bargains at the bottom enables you to keep your well-selected stock in place without worry and to use options to gain profits no matter which way the stock price moves. With swing trading, the specific timing of the trades helps you to maximize your option-based profits with minimal risk, and to create greater short-term profits from the extreme emotions of the market. Greed, fear, and uncertainty can do great damage to your portfolio if you allow them to rule your decisions. Using swing trading as part of your overall strategy, you can steer clear of those emotionally troubled waters and profit in all types of markets.

As sensible as swing trading is for taking advantage of short-term overreactions, profitable trading creates profits, and that means the government will want its share. When it comes to options, the complexities of the U.S. Tax Code become extreme. If you are not aware of some special rules, you can actually lose long-term status for stock you own, so you need to know the rules before you trade. The rules for options are complex and odd. Chapter 8 explains how federal taxes work in the options market.

TAX RULES FOR OPTIONS

*"Man is not like other animals in the ways that are really significant;
animals have instincts, we have taxes."*
—Erving Goffman, in the *New York Times*, February 12, 1969

OST PEOPLE WILL AGREE that the U.S. Tax Code is complex. But if you think you have seen the worst of it with your personal return, think again. The rules for taxation of options are probably among the most complicated in the Internal Revenue Code (IRC).

Most tax rules have come about for good reasons, and option rules are no exception. When members of Congress enacted the latest changes to the rules for option taxes, they were attempting to curtail the use of options to defer taxes, but it only made the rules even more mind-boggling for everyone. However, if you are aware of the rules and limitations, you can avoid the most common mistakes and get through your tax return with minimal trouble. Your biggest concern should not be completing the tax return but making mistakes during the year. A seemingly easy decision—for example, rolling forward with a covered call— could trigger the loss of long-term capital gains status for stock, no matter how long you have owned it. There can be some severe and expensive consequences if you do not know the rules.

Once you understand how the option tax rules work, you can use those rules to maximize profits, use up carry-over losses, and avoid unintended tax penalties resulting from poor timing.

Capital Gains Rules

Every investor should be very familiar with capital gains tax rules. The rate of tax you pay on your stock profits is going to be determined by how long you own the stock, so part of your portfolio planning process should include an awareness of tax benefits or consequences.

Whenever you sell stock or options, you report the net profit or loss as a *capital gain or loss*. This is distinguished from "ordinary" income by the way it is taxed and by annual limitations on the deductibility of losses. If you own assets for 12 months or fewer, your gains are taxed at the same rates as your other income. If you own assets longer than 12 months, the maximum tax rate on net gains is 15 percent, at least through the end of 2008 (future revisions may change this rate for later years). The definition of "net gains" is the difference between long-term gains and short-term losses.

When options are involved in calculation of capital gains and losses, the whole issue gets complicated. When you buy long options, the same rules apply as those for other capital assets. So if the holding period is less than 12 months and you sell the option, it is a short-term gain. If your holding period is longer than 12 months, it is treated as a long-term gain or loss when you sell. This rule applies to options you buy and then close, and not to exercised long options.

When you exercise, the rule is different. If you buy a call and it is automatically exercised or if you exercise it yourself, the net profit or loss is treated as part of your basis in stock.

EXAMPLE

If you buy a call and pay 3 ($300) and later buy 100 shares of stock at the strike price of $25 per share, your basis in that stock is $2,800. The holding period of stock in this case begins on the day after exercise.

If you own a long put and exercise it, the cost of the put is deducted from the exercise price of stock you sell.

EXAMPLE

If you bought a put for 4 ($400) with a strike of 25 to insure stock you owned worth $28 per share, your intention was to prevent losing money if and when the stock's value declined. If the stock's value fell to $19 per share and you exercised your put, you would sell at the strike of 25, but your net proceeds would be $21 per share. The net would be treated as a long-term or short-term gain depending on the holding period of the stock.

When you sell an option and receive proceeds, you are not taxed. The tax applies in the year the option expires, is exercised, or is closed. All short options are treated as short-term no matter how long the holding period. If a short call is exercised, your tax is calculated by adding the strike price to the premium. The same rule applies to short puts: They are always treated as short-term gains or losses.

If a buyer exercises your short put and you are required to buy 100 shares at the strike, your basis is the strike price, and your holding period begins the day after exercise. And your short put becomes a short-term capital gain.

It is usually true that gains or losses are treated as taxable in the year positions are closed. This has always been a basis rule of the tax code. There is one exception, though, and that is the straddle. The IRS defines a straddle's segments as *offsetting positions*. This means that under the usual tax treatment, it would be possible to experience a net loss one year and a profit the next. For tax planning reasons, this could be a desirable outcome. However, under the offsetting positions limitations, some losses cannot be deducted until the entire straddle has been closed.

This raises some difficult questions. For example, what if you open a covered call and later open a second position that creates a straddle? Does the offsetting positions rule apply? The answer is uncertain. When these kinds of adjustments are made to the tax rules, they often cause more problems than they solve.

There are four possible ways that straddle taxes might be adjusted:

1. In some cases, the long-term period of stock could be suspended for as long as the straddle remains open. For example, if you have owned stock for eight months, your normal long-term window would begin four months later. However, if you open a straddle and it remains open for six months, you might not be able to claim a long-term gain. The time period to reach the required 12 months is suspended while the position is left open.

2. The wash sale rule (discussed later in this chapter) might be applied against a loss in one side of the straddle.

3. Any current deductions could be deferred until the remaining position—called the "successor position"—is closed.

4. The current cost of the straddle (margin interest and brokerage fees) could be deferred and deducted only when the successor position is closed.

A special rule also applies to a so-called *married put*. This is a put purchased to insure long stock. However, if you buy a put on the same day that you buy stock and it expires or gets exercised, it may be treated as an adjustment in the basis of stock. If the put is later closed, it is still treated separately, as a short-term capital gain.

Some Tax Law Oddities

THE WASH SALE RULE

You have probably heard of the *wash sale rule*, but in all likelihood, you have not thought about its ramifications for options. The rule states that if you sell stock and buy it again within 30 days, you cannot deduct a loss.

Before the wash sale rule was in effect, a year-end planning device involved selling stock held at a loss, waiting for the new year, and repurchasing the stock. This had the effect of creating a current-year loss. It could be used to offset other gains during the year or simply to create a loss carryover to be used in the future. Now, however, under the wash sale rule, if you reopen a stock position within 30 days, the loss is eliminated.

You can still use the strategy by selling loss-position stock near the end of the year, and then repurchasing the same number of sales—as long as at least 31 days have passed. Some option traders might immediately come up with a solution: sell stock and buy an in-the-money put. If the put is exercised, the stock comes back into the portfolio and the wash sale rule is avoided. However, this does not work. Under the tax rules, using in-the-money puts to avoid the wash sale rule will eliminate the loss just as if you had sold and repurchased stock within 30 days.

Some investors worry that the stock might rise within the 30-day restriction period. To offset that threat, you might consider buying a long call in the stock, a form of insurance against price rises that also locks in a strike price if you want to get back into the position after the 30-day period has expired. However, if you do end up exercising the long call and repurchasing the stock, there is also a possibility that the IRS will interpret this as another version of the wash sale.

One place where the wash sale rule does not matter is in an IRA (individual retirement account) or other tax-deferred account. Under retirement account rules, no profits are taxed until you begin taking withdrawals. Even if a transaction were treated as a wash sale, it would have no effect on IRA value. For example, if you simply want to move out of loss-position stock near the end of the year in the belief that its value is going to continue declining after December 31, you can execute a sale and then repurchase. It does not matter if you do so within the 30-day wash sale period because no tax will apply. However, situations in which such a wash sale would be profitable are limited. The fact is that most people exiting a position in December and reentering it in January are going to be motivated by tax concerns.

The wash sale rule might strike you as an oddity, but it

serves a purpose. Like many tax rules, it was designed to prevent people from creating losses this year and deferring gains until later. In theory, if you had a huge portfolio, you could eliminate a lot of tax liability simply by playing the timing of booking your losses. The wash sale rule prevents this.

CONSTRUCTIVE SALES RULES

In the options market, you also have to be concerned about *constructive sales rules*. Under the IRC, a constructive sale is created even when you do not execute a sale order. You might create an unintentional constructive sale when you open offsetting long and short positions using options or stock.

EXAMPLE

You bought 100 shares of stock at $35, and today it is valued at $50. You do not want to take profits this year, but you believe the stock's price is going to decline, so you sell 100 shares short. Although these positions may be considered entirely different, the IRS might call this transaction a constructive sale. If so, the $35 stock sold at $50 would create a capital gain of $1,500.

A constructive sale might also occur when you use options to work a stock portfolio in one of the many ways discussed in previous chapters. For example, say you buy 100 shares at $35 and later, when the stock is at $50, you buy a put for insurance. The determination of whether this becomes a constructive sale depends on the timing of both transactions, the final outcome of trades, and the actual price movement in stock and option. If you are going to embark on a program of using options to strategically insure or enhance your portfolio, you need to discuss the potential tax ramifications with a tax professional.

RULES ON CARRYOVER LOSSES

Another area where options can be used strategically involves carryover losses. This is yet another area where the tax rules are illogical, an outgrowth of good intentions that have created a complex and irrational result.

Under the tax rules, the maximum capital loss you can deduct per year is $3,000. If you have a net loss above this level, you have to apply it to future years, where it can be used to offset capital gains or slowly depleted at the rate of $3,000 per year. For many people, this has created a large burden. If you lost money during the era of corporate scandals in companies like Enron, WorldCom, or Tyco (to name a few), chances are you have a substantial capital loss carryover—and chances are also that you do not see any prospects of absorbing the entire loss in your lifetime. However, the options market offers you a solution. One of the most important and restrictive tax rules concerns qualified versus unqualified covered calls.

QUALIFIED COVERED CALLS: COMPLICATING THE ISSUES

Anyone who writes in-the-money covered calls has to be aware of one of the strangest rules in the tax code: a distinction between "qualified" and "unqualified" covered calls. Under this rule, if you write a covered call too deep in the money, you lose the long-term capital gains status of your stock. The definition of "qualified" includes stock price levels, time to expiration, and the strike price of the covered call.

EXAMPLE

If you bought stock 11 months ago at $20 and it is now worth $30, the simple act of writing an unqualified call means that if the stock is called away, you might have to pay the full tax rate as though it were a short-term gain *even if you end up owning the stock more than one full year.* Of course, each call written as an unqualified call restricts only 100 shares of stock in this manner. And chances of exercise are high because an unqualified call, by definition, is deep in the money. Table 8-1 summarizes the levels at which calls have to be written to qualify (meaning to keep long-term gains status) for stock at various prices and with various terms until expiration.

TABLE 8-1. QUALIFIED COVERED CALLS.

The previous day's closing price of stock	Time left until expiration	Strike price limitations
$25 or less	over 30 days	One strike price under the previous day's closing price of stock (one exception: a qualified call cannot have a strike price less than 85% of the stock's price)
$25.01 to $60	over 30 days	One strike price under the previous day's closing price of stock
$60.01 to $150	31–90 days	One strike price under the previous day's closing price of stock
$60.01 to $150	over 90 days	Two strike prices under the previous day's closing price of stock (however, not more than 10 points in the money)
$150.01 or more	31–90 days	One strike price under the previous day's closing price of stock
$150.01 or more	over 90 days	Two strike prices under the previous day's closing price of stock

The complexity of these rules may be troubling, but as a general rule, you will be writing an unqualified covered call if it is beyond one strike price in the money (compared with the previous trading day's close). If you write an unqualified call, any long-term capital gains you have in the stock (in other words, when you have owned the stock a year or more) are in jeopardy.

The rule affects your status in the following ways:

- *There is no change for at-the-money or out-of-the-money covered calls.* The distinction between qualified and unqualified applies only to in-the-money covered calls. As long as your covered calls are within one strike price of the past day's close, or at or in the money, you will not lose your long-term status for stock.

- *Qualified in-the-money calls are not affected.* As long as you keep your in-the-money covered calls within that strike price and expiration window (shown in Table 8-1), your covered call will be qualified.

- *Long-term capital gains are affected for all unqualified covered calls.* The period counting up to the one-year requirement to qualify for long-term capital gains is suspended during the time the unqualified covered call is written. Because it is deep in the money, there is a better than average chance it will be exercised. If you owned stock for 11 months and 29 days or *less* at the time you write an unqualified covered call, the exercise of stock will be short-term even if it takes place after that period.

You might intend to avoid unqualified covered calls based on the oddity of these rules, but say you end up with one unintentionally. Perhaps you own 100 shares of stock you originally bought 11 months ago at $45. The stock closed yesterday at $58 per share. You had sold a 50 call two months ago when the stock was at $49 per share, and today you want to roll out of that position. You buy the 50 and sell a later-expiring 52.50 covered call. However, this simple roll forward and up has created an unqualified call, because the stock closed yesterday at $58, which means that to qualify you would have to have sold a 55 or 57.50 call.

The consequence of this example is that the count to long-term capital gains is suspended at the 11-month point. If the 52.50 call is exercised, you will have to pay the full ordinary tax rate on the stock profit, because the unqualified covered call suspended the count. This is one example of how you can unintentionally fall into the unqualified zone without intending to.

If you experience losses on covered calls—even those that are qualified—they are treated as long-term losses when the underlying stock has met the conditions to be treated as long-term gains. In other words, the long-term rules for these related profits and losses are to be matched. Thus, you would not be able to create a highly favorable situation in which your gains were taxed as long-term, but you also get the benefits of short-term losses.

The troubling issue of the stock's holding period is also complicated when you sell the covered call. If you sell a call at a loss, the wash sale rule applies; you have to hold the stock an additional 30 days in order for the call to be treated as qualified.

As disheartening and complicated as the qualified rule is, the rule also offers you a strategic opportunity. There are three situations in which you will not be concerned about the question of qualification and in which it can even be an advantage. These are:

1. *You intend to sell stock before the long-term period.* If you plan to dispose of your stock before a one-year

holding period would take effect, the question of qualification does not concern you. Even without the restriction, you intend to create a short-term gain by selling stock before the question arises. This raises an interesting strategic possibility. It is often the case that you intend to sell stock before a one-year holding period is met, and at the same time, you believe there is a chance the stock's price is going to dip. In this situation, selling a deep in-the-money call is unqualified but could create additional income. If you are right and the stock's price falls, the covered call can be closed at a profit, opening an additional avenue for short-term income.

2. *You are writing covered calls within a qualified retirement plan.* When you are writing covered calls within an IRA or other qualified retirement plan, all of your income is free of tax until later, when you begin taking withdrawals. When you do begin withdrawing, all of the proceeds are treated as ordinary income, so capital gains are not an issue. In this situation, you can write calls as deep in the money as you want, because there are no tax consequences.

3. *You have a large carryover loss and you want short-term gains for offset.* The most interesting of possible strategies involves the case where you have a large carryover loss. The only way this loss will be absorbed is by being offset against future profits. It is reasonable to say that in this situation, current income from investments is going to be sheltered by the carryover loss. So even with a very large loss, you can apply current-year profits against those losses and pay no tax on them. With this situation, you may not be concerned with the question of whether gains are short-term or long-term, or whether you write qualified or unqualified covered calls.

▣   Coordinating Options in Your Larger Portfolio Plan

The tax rules make options exceptionally complex and demand careful planning to avoid unexpected consequences. However, this is merely a planning aspect to keep in mind and should not be a reason for you to avoid the profit potential of options. Here are some important planning guidelines:

- *Never make decisions based on tax consequences above and beyond profits.* It is amazing that, simply to reduce their tax burden, people will at times create bigger expenses or even avoid profits. For example, you might be able to afford to pay off your mortgage but fail to do so because you don't want to lose the itemized deduction for interest. But the math doesn't support this decision. Why spend $10,000 per year to get a $3,500 tax benefit? You would be better off with no interest expense and an after-tax savings of $6,500. The same observation applies to stocks and options. Your priority should be to create profits within your portfolio using whatever strategies work for you and conform to your risk tolerance level. If this includes options, it would make no sense at all to avoid them because the taxes are complicated.

- *Study and compare before deciding.* The best way to profit from options is to become familiar with how a specific action is going to be taxed. By analyzing how a transaction is going to work on an after-tax basis, you are more likely to make informed decisions and maximize current income.

- *Become familiar with the rules before entering or exiting a trade.* So many people enter option trades without thinking about the consequences because they just don't know what they are. For example, you might end up paying much more in taxes than necessary by the mere timing of a trade or selection of an option—a problem that is easily avoided if you know the rules.

- *Keep the specifics in mind, especially if you have a large carryover loss.* The problem of unqualified call writing is an issue only if you are going to be hit with extra taxes as the result of your decisions. If you have a large carryover loss, you are not going to be taxed on the profits from call exercise, even if unqualified; your carryover loss acts as a shelter for as long as it lasts, freeing you to earn as much short-term capital gains income as you can. This often leads investors to prefer deep in-the-money covered calls to force exercise *and* create current income (and, at the same time, create potential additional current income if the stock's value and in-the-money call decline in value before exercise).

- *Check with a professional to make sure you know the consequences of your decisions.* Not everyone is going to be willing to take the time to become an expert in the complexities of option taxes. This is why tax attorneys and accountants have job security. It is smart to pay for tax planning advice *before* the end of the year and before you begin making a series of trades in your portfolio. Before embarking on a program of aggressive straddle and covered call writing strategies, review your ideas with a tax professional and make sure you know how it will come out. The worst time to be surprised is when you see the "amount due" line on your tax return.

Options—even with their complex tax rules—provide you with many ways to protect your portfolio and even to turn it into a great cash generator. In fact, options open many doors for you, including the ability to diversify in a new and rewarding way: by strategy instead of by stock. Chapter 9 examines the whole topic of diversification with options as part of the equation.

DIVERSIFYING BY STRATEGY INSTEAD OF BY STOCK

"He that wants money, means and content is without three good friends."
—William Shakespeare, *As You Like It*, 1599

ANY PORTFOLIO MANAGEMENT POLICY has to include the question "How do you reduce risk?" The two primary purposes of portfolio management are planning for the future through selection of appropriate stocks, and controlling or reducing today's risks. The two purposes are directly related; however, many investors are aware only of the most apparent and immediate risks. To effectively manage a long-term portfolio, you also need to analyze a *range* of risks you face merely by having open positions in the market.

Most people acknowledge the concept that diversification reduces risk. But not *all* kinds of diversification adequately reduce *all* kinds of risk. The risks you face in your portfolio come in a variety of forms. Anticipating these various risks is the key to creating the kind of growth you need in your portfolio and to reduce the chances for unexpected (and costly) surprises. This chapter explains the many kinds of risk you face in your portfolio and shows how an option program can serve as one strategic tool for reaching your personal goals while remaining true to your risk tolerance limits.

Identifying Specific Risks

Unfortunately for many investors, there are two levels of risk: the actual risks to which a portfolio is exposed, versus the risks an investor believes are present. The gap between these two is often quite wide.

For example, although many people describe themselves as conservative or moderate, or base their investment philosophy on the fundamentals, when it comes time to actually trade, they act and react very technically, often taking higher risks than they can afford. These market risks tend to be based on price movement on stocks, and all too often the decision to buy or sell is based on the recommendation of a friend, co-worker, or television financial show. As a consequence, it is quite easy to place money in the wrong place. Any decisions made without in-depth research is likely to lead to such problems, because no investor should make a specific decision without matching the stock to his/her risk profile.

This basic observation is worth repeating because the mistake is so common. Avoid these three mistakes in the way you make decisions in the market:

1. *Reacting in the moment without a view to the long term.* For some investors, the market becomes a daily obsession or game. The excitement of entering trades or tak-

ing profits leads to an "act and react" format for investing. There is a name for this: speculation. So even a very conservative value investor who has picked stocks for long-term growth is likely to take profits with a small point increase and to move in and out of stocks, often at the worst possible time. The same tendency leads to some generalizations about the market that are untrue or that lead you away from the fundamentals. For example, you might have heard that "when a stock goes up 2 points, it always goes up 2 more points on the next trading day." Another belief: "Forget about buy low and sell high; buy high and sell higher."

These generalizations work in some kinds of markets and for some kinds of stocks, but remember the philosophy of the fundamental investor: *Buy the company, not the stock*. If you believe a company has exceptional chances for long-term growth, and it dominates its industry competitively with an exceptional management team, it does not matter what the stock does from day to day. A good approach to the market is to buy bargain-priced value companies, and then use options to work short-term prices.

2. Depending on television financial news shows for major investment moves. With increasing regularity, the television news show has become the new brokerage office for American investors. In ancient times (the 1970s and 1980s), investors had to visit a downtown brokerage office to follow a ticker tape or speak with a broker. In fact, they could not even make a trade without running it through their stockbroker. Today, trading is much easier, and along with that, advice is free and can be found everywhere.

The problem with this approach to investing is twofold. First, you don't know the assumption base underlying a recommendation. Second, even if those assumptions are explained, it does not necessarily mean that the recommended company is a good match for your portfolio. There are too many variables.

3. *Buying or selling solely in reaction to price movement.* Trading is fun. The movement of real money in and out of trades, often in the thousands of dollars, is exhilarating, and for a good reason: There is risk involved. Obviously, you cannot earn profits without taking risks, and every realistic investor accepts this as a reality. However, the decision to buy or sell shares of stock should be based on a series of analytical conclusions conforming to your risk profile, the market and other risks involved, and the actual value of the stock.

Your risk profile might rely on long-term value companies, meaning that if you buy or sell based only on price changes in the stock, you are speculating and not investing. That contradicts your self-defined risk profile. Knowing the risks involved with a specific decision should be the starting point, but it often is overlooked completely. Finally, the *value* of the stock is crucial because you probably want to pick up stocks at a bargain price. The idea of "buy low and sell high" (or the alternative, "buy high and sell higher") is not always applicable. Some companies will experience a big run-up in stock price and still be a bargain; others will look cheap but, based on the fundamentals, will not represent bargains. The common practice of trading on small-point increments can be dangerous. It belongs more effectively in the realm of swing trading using options and should be excluded from the trading of stock.

A brief study of the various kinds of market risk is worth your time, if only as a review of what you already know. With all of the temptations of the market, including the allure of fast and frequent trades, it pays to step back and look at the question of risk. It may save you the expensive mistake of trading for all of the wrong reasons.

Market Risk

The well-known *market risk* is simply the risk that a stock's value will fall after you buy. Put another way, many buyers have an unspoken assumption that their entry point into a stock is "ground zero" and that the price is going to rise from that point. This is a common belief, but a dangerous one.

The fact is that any price at which you buy stock is not a zero level, but a midrange price. This means that the price can move either up or down. Of course, you know this. But are you operating on the knowledge, or are you acting as a ground zero investor? This is an important question to ask yourself because the false assumption can and does lead to problems later on. For example, if you buy stock the day before it tumbles 10 percent, it could take weeks or even months for the value to get back to the point of entry, or ground zero for that stock. To appreciate market risk, you also need to understand that the price you pay is not a starting point.

Market risk is misunderstood by the predominantly optimistic investor. The very idea that the price could move *below* your purchase price is unthinkable, especially if you did all of the fundamental and technical analysis you needed to do. No matter how thoroughly you test, what kind of price targets you set, or what signals you pick up, your timing is not always going to be perfect. This is why it is called market *risk*. There are no guarantees that your timing will be perfect or even correct every time. So as an investor, you have to live with this risk. The problem is not with the existence of market risk but with the fact that so many investors pretend it is not there.

The coordination of your portfolio with market risk can be greatly improved with the use of options. You can think of market risk as containing a series of short-term temptations. As soon as a stock's price rises, the first question is: *"Should I take profits now while they are available?"* If the price falls, the opposite question prevails: *"Should I cut my losses before the price falls even more?"*

To resist the temptations that accompany short-term market risk, you must rely on maintaining your long-term perspective. If that sounds like an obvious statement, consider how easy it is to act contrary to this approach. A lot of the price correction action in the market is derived from taking profits and cutting losses. In other words, investors tend to buy high and sell low because they invariably misread market risk.

Some value investors belief they should buy stock and forget about it. They avoid reading financial newspapers or watching financial television shows. However, while it is wise to *not* transact too often or at the wrong times, ignoring stock doesn't make any sense, either. Even the strongest company today can lose its edge in the future. Consider some of the most prestigious corporations of only a few years ago: American Airlines and United Airlines, General Motors and Ford, or Kodak and Polaroid, to name a few. Because the economy and technology have changed, today's value investment will change in the future as well. Companies, like industries, move ahead or fall back as technology changes. Only a few decades ago, the computer industry didn't even exist. Microsoft and Apple were not yet founded, and IBM was a typewriter company.

In understanding the ramifications of market risk, you also need to recognize that the whole market is evolving. It may be that in the near future, global tests of corporate strength will dominate the market, and today's domestic emphasis will be obsolete and even meaningless. Future inventions will also change the risk factors. So in any study of market risk, you also need to acknowledge that the market itself is changing. In the 19th century, the dominant companies were railroads and big banks funding construction of canals. In the 20th century, U.S. auto manufacturers and airlines were among the most powerful companies. In the early 21st century, IT holds an edge, at least for the moment.

Market risk is not an unchanging force, which is why you cannot afford to just buy today's value company and forget about it. With each change in technology and emergence of global forces, you need to reevaluate your portfolio. This is how you manage and reduce market risk.

In the meantime, you can use market risk to your advantage with options. Assuming your portfolio consists of carefully selected, high-value companies with excellent growth potential, you can employ a series of specific option strategies—such as insurance, covered calls, and swing trading—to act as a contrarian and to create current income. In other words, you can exploit the reaction of most investors to actual market risk by entering a series of carefully timed trades aimed at protecting your portfolio and increasing current income.

Collateral Risk

One form of risk often overlooked by investors (especially those using options) is *collateral risk*. You can transact business on credit using your margin account, but the more you buy and sell on margin, the greater your overall risk. Brokerage firms make it all too easy and, in fact, automatic, for investors to have access to margin accounts.

If you deposit $10,000 with an online firm and apply for margin trading, you will receive an additional $10,000 of credit. This means essentially that you can leverage your capital to double your profits. Unfortunately, you can *more than double* your losses as well.

For example, with that $10,000 at risk, you face the normal market risks everyone does. But if you lose on a $20,000 investment portfolio, you double the potential losses—you still have to repay the $10,000 borrowed from your brokerage firm, as well as interest on the borrowed funds.

Using margins entails risks not visible at the time you enter positions. If the market value of your open long positions falls or if the value of open short positions rises, you are going to be required to deposit more money. This is required by a federal law to maintain the 50-50 at-risk requirement. The Federal Reserve's Regulation T states that you can borrow up to 50 percent of the price of securities as an initial margin. However, you must maintain that 50 percent requirement no matter how prices change. If you are unable to meet margin calls, your brokerage firm has the right to sell securities in your portfolio without your permission. This is one of the risks of margin investing.

Some people look at the almost automatic margin provision as easy credit and recognize the potential profit without also understanding the potential risk. The solution is to use options to create attractive leverage in place of margin. Options allow you to control 100 shares of stock per contract, for a small fraction of what 100 shares would cost; and while options do expire in the future, there is no interest obligation or margin call involved. If you want to leverage your portfolio, you need to understand collateral risk and to compare the advantages and risks of margin investing and options.

Margin accounts can be used effectively for temporary

financing, or for a type of "bridge loan" when you expect to be short of cash for only a few days.

EXAMPLE

You plan to sell stock as soon as your current covered call expires, which is this Friday. You plan to enter a sell order first thing Monday morning. The call is out of the money, and you doubt that the stock will rise enough to be exercised. Meanwhile, you want to buy stock in a different company, and you would prefer to buy now rather than wait until funds are available from the sale you expect to make next Monday. In this situation, you can use your margin account to buy shares now, even though you have not yet sold shares on which you have a covered call. You will be charged less than one week's interest. As long as this is worthwhile to you, going in and out of your margin account is acceptable.

Margin accounts are also handy for those using options in the very short term, such as within a swing trading strategy.

EXAMPLE

A stock has risen substantially and you have spotted a sell set-up. Using options, you want to buy puts (rather than selling the stock short) in anticipation of the stock's price falling over the next three to five days. There is no cash available in your fully-invested portfolio. In this situation, your margin account is a very convenient vehicle for funding your swing trading trades, given that you do not intend to keep positions open for more than a few days.

Whenever you use your margin account, remember that it is a form of borrowing and that those borrowed funds have to be repaid with interest. Using margin to invest is a greater risk than an all-cash approach, because the profit potential is accompanied by an equal loss potential. As long as you understand the scope of collateral risk, the margin account is a wonderful convenience. The wisest approach is to use it only to bridge very short-term shortfalls.

Personal Goals Risk

Another form of invisible risk for many investors is *personal goals risk*. This is the risk that you might make trades contrary to your own goals or outside of your risk tolerance. All investors are susceptible to this risk. It is easy to get distracted from the portfolio goals and characteristics that you established for yourself when you began investing, and end up chasing profits through short-term speculation. You might also buy the wrong stocks as part of this problem. Here are some worthwhile guidelines:

- *Remember the fundamentals of the company.* It invariably pays to make a clear distinction between the stock and the company. As previously stated, one of the numerous Wall Street adages advises you to "buy the company, not the stock." This has a specific meaning. The only way to spot bargains is to understand the fundamentals—the capitalization, working capital, and earnings power behind the numbers. If you focus on the stock and how its market value changes by a few points per week, you are prevented from looking at the fundamentals, so the underlying value may become unimportant within the price-focused scheme of things. That's when mistakes start to occur.

- *Never allow yourself to pick stocks based on option values.* Options are very alluring, and many once-conservative investors become high-risk speculators because they have a delusional belief that options solve all problems. Options are cheap, they can be used to double an investment in a matter of days or even hours, and they are safer than stocks. But you need to maintain a perspective on options and how they fit with the rest of your portfolio. Stocks should continue to form the core of your long-term plan because you need to build growth and value over time. Options work best as a tool for managing your portfolio, but not as a substitute for good stock selection.

- *Be a value investor for the long term; use options to create income for the short term.* The best possible use of options is as a secondary strategic application within the larger portfolio itself. Your value-based selection of companies should always dominate within your portfolio, and options should never serve as a substitute for that. When options are used to take short-term profits without affecting your portfolio, to maximize price opportunities after share value falls, to insure positions, and to create additional cash income (through covered call writing, for example), you are able to maintain your position as a long-term value investor. At the same time, you can improve overall profitability while reducing risks. That is where options can become valuable as part of your value-based portfolio.

- *Revisit your investment goals and risk tolerance regularly.* Remember that the specific investment goals you set and the carefully developed risk tolerance levels that guide your decisions are both subject to change. In fact, change is inevitable. Any major change in your personal life is going to change your goals. This includes starting a new job, marriage, birth of a child, divorce, losing a job, a major relocation or career change, or the death of a loved one. All of these events are significant and are going to change your goals, sometimes drastically. In addition, your age and income can and do alter your specific investment profile.

As you gain experience as an investor, your risk tolerance levels are likely to change as well. There is a tendency for younger, less experienced investors to be attracted to higher profit (and risk) investments, and for older, more experienced investors to become increasingly conservative. These are generalizations, of course. However, whatever your risk tolerance level is today, once you discover the potential in options, it is likely that your appreciation of risk itself is going to change significantly. You may discover methods to increase current income while adding greater protection to your long stock positions.

Personal goals risk is one of those most overlooked. There is a tendency for investors to make broad generalizations and for investment advisers to operate on many broad assumptions. If you listen carefully to television financial programs, you note that most discussions focus on predictions about the price direction of companies. Very seldom do you hear television advisers discuss risk factors such as volatility of a stock, financial instability of the company itself, or suitability for some types of portfolios. These are issues that you need to address for yourself, to determine what kinds of risks are appropriate for you. That is where your personal goals become so important. If you cannot afford to take market risks and you end up in some very volatile stocks, that violates your personal goals and risk tolerance.

■ The Risk of an Unavailable Market

Before online trading dominated the markets, the risk of an "unavailable market" was a more serious one than it is today. In those days, when most individuals placed trades with a stockbroker, high-volume days meant that telephone lines were jammed and it was impossible for everyone to get through.

Let's look at two days when the market was unavailable, for very different reasons. On October 19, 1987, the Dow Jones Industrial Average (DJIA) fell 508 points. The one-day fall, known as Black Monday, was at that point the biggest one-day drop in stock market history. This can be compared to what happened on September 17, 2001—six days after the 9/11 attacks. The markets, which had been closed on 9/11, reopened that day—and the DJIA fell 685 points.

There is a significant difference between these two events. In 1987, there was no Internet to speak of. The Internet did not really become available to the public until the 1990s, which ultimately opened the doors to innovations such as online discount brokerage and direct access to stock trading.

On October 19, 1987, everyone depended on the now-obsolete stockbroker and the use of a telephone. While the one-day panic was in full force, most people were unable to get through to their stockbroker, and they could not cut their losses. Since those days, exchanges have instituted automatic trading stops to avoid one-day panics. But even without that change in the rules, the pre-Internet days were likely to experience many situations when markets simply were not available.

Following the September 11, 2001 attacks, the markets closed for several days—another form of an unavailable market. Even with the Internet, this was simply unavoidable because of the breakdown in basic communications that occurred. The New York exchanges had backup systems so data was not lost, but there were no basic communications based on telephones and electricity. In addition, it was impossible for stock exchange employees to even get to work during the week following the attacks, so the markets were closed out of necessity. However, once they opened and the DJIA fell 685 points, everyone with a computer was able to get quotes and execute trades online, without the need for stockbrokers or telephones. This made a substantial difference in the sense that the Internet had eliminated the bottleneck that previously existed when the telephone was the primary means—and for many, the only means—for placing trades.

Today, markets can become unavailable for more mundane reasons. Something as simple as a blackout means you cannot turn on your computer. If you depend on a telephone connection, a break in phone service has the same effect. Hopefully, there will not be an extensive multi-day blackout affecting large areas of the country in the future, but the possibility surely exists. Catastrophic events like major hurricanes, earthquakes, and other natural disasters will also disrupt markets.

The "unavailability" of a market has a different meaning to some. For example, some investments lack a secondary market so that holdings cannot be sold in an auction like the stock market. If you have purchased units in limited partnerships and you want to sell, you will probably have to take a large discount because of the unavailability of a market. Stocks traded over exchanges are highly liquid, and the auction is a daily reality. So other than those days when programmed trading stops take place or the exchanges are closed (or disasters disrupt communications), the stock market is perhaps the most liquid and available venue available.

The risk of an unavailable market remains a reality, but it tends to disappear within a few days. When you consider the disruptions created in the 9/11 attacks, it is amazing that the markets were closed for only one week. Those disruptions included not only destruction of buildings and loss of life but downed telephone and computer services over a wide area—which also happens to be the Wall Street complex that serves as the center for the U.S. stock markets. So even such a serious disruption in trading lasted for what was actually a very short time period.

Tax and Inflation Risks

Another form of risk often overlooked by investors is the double effect of taxes and inflation. Even with relatively low rates of both of these, the overall impact on your after-tax, after-inflation net earnings can be substantial. For many investors who own stocks yielding 1 or 2 percent in dividends per year, this type of risk can mean you are losing "real money" when both of these forces are taken into account.

To calculate your "breakeven" point (where you neither profit nor lose), divide the current inflation rate by your net after-tax income rate (100 minus your effective tax rate, including both federal and state tax rates you pay). The formula is:

$$\frac{I}{100 - R} = B$$

I = *rate of inflation*
R = *effective tax rate (federal and state)*
B = *breakeven return*

Table 9-1 provides a chart for showing the after-tax, after-inflation breakeven rate at various percentages.

For example, if the current rate of inflation is 2 percent (you find this by checking the Consumer Price Index at www.bea.gov), you would use the second column in Table 9-1 (under "2%"). Next, find your "effective tax rate." This is the rate you pay in tax. To find this rate, divide your total annual tax liability by your taxable income. Be sure to add together the federal and state rates. For example, if you pay 15 percent on federal and an additional 5 percent state income tax, your effective tax rate is 20 percent. Putting this another way, it is the rate you pay on all income you earn above your current income. With a 20 percent effective tax rate and 2 percent inflation, your breakeven point is 2.5 percent.

This means you need to earn 2.5 percent on your investments just to maintain. So one-half percent will go to

TABLE 9-1. AFTER-TAX, AFTER-INFLATION BREAKEVEN RATES.

Effective tax rate	Inflation Rate					
	1%	2%	3%	4%	5%	6%
14%	1.2%	2.3%	3.5%	4.7%	5.8%	7.0%
16%	1.2	2.4	3.6	4.8	6.0	7.1
18%	1.2	2.4	3.7	4.9	6.1	7.3
20%	1.3	2.5	3.8	5.0	6.3	7.5
22%	1.3	2.6	3.8	5.1	6.4	7.7
24%	1.3%	2.6%	3.9%	5.3%	6.6%	7.9%
26%	1.4	2.7	4.1	5.4	6.8	8.1
28%	1.4	2.8	4.2	5.6	6.9	8.3
30%	1.4	2.9	4.3	5.7	7.1	8.6
32%	1.5	2.9	4.4	5.9	7.4	8.8
34%	1.5%	3.0%	4.5%	6.1%	7.6%	9.1%
36%	1.6	3.1	4.7	6.3	7.8	9.4
38%	1.6	3.2	4.8	6.5	8.1	9.7
40%	1.7	3.3	5.0	6.7	8.3	10.0
42%	1.7	3.4	5.2	6.9	8.6	10.3

income taxes (2.5% x 20% = 0.5%). That leaves an after-tax profit of 2 percent, which is equal to the inflation rate. Thus, in order to truly improve your investment portfolio value, your net has to be greater than 2.5 percent. If you own stocks that do not increase in value and the dividend yield is under 2.5 percent, you are losing money.

This is where options can vastly improve your portfolio's performance. In previous chapters, many option strategies—notably covered call writing—have been shown to create far greater profits, often in double digits. And these profits are created without added market risk. So you can create net returns far above your breakeven point and maintain your risk profile at the same time. Your tax liability will be higher, but you still come out ahead. Even with a 20 percent tax burden, your after-tax option profits will remain at a net of 80 percent of the pre-tax yield. (For example, for every $100 earned from options, $20 would represent an increased tax liability, and $80 an after-tax profit.) In this situation, more income equals higher taxes *and* higher after-tax income.

Breakeven calculation is important because some investors are completely unaware that they are losing money on their low-yielding stocks. It is often an invisible risk. Risk assessment has to take the double impact of taxes and inflation into account. Many people believe that they are conservative and, as a result, they pick low-volatility stocks with little or no market risk (and little or no dividend yield or price movement). The real outcome of this "safe" investment strategy is the loss of spending power over time, as a conservative portfolio's value is eroded by even a small rate of inflation and minimal actual returns as a result of income tax liabilities.

Once you are aware of the minimum return you need in order to break even after taxes and inflation, you are better suited to evaluate your portfolio. What was your overall return last year? Was it greater than your break-even rate? If so, one solution is to revisit your market risk analysis in line with the stocks you hold and question whether your portfolio is a rational match for you. Another solution is to consider whether or not options can be used to ensure that you always beat your breakeven point.

▪ Lost Opportunity Risk

Perhaps the most significant risk involved with option-based strategies is the lost opportunity risk. Assuming that you employ only the most conservative of strategies, such as covered call writing, there is always the possibility that you will lose out on *higher* profits if you do not use options.

Covered call writers make a trade. They create situations in which double-digit returns are certain, regardless of outcome, and in exchange they accept lost opportunity risk. For example, you might buy stock and write calls, gaining dividend income as well as premium from the calls you sell. If the calls are selected properly, exercise creates a capital gain on top of the short call premium and dividend income. If the call expires worthless, you are free to write another. If the call's value declines, you can buy to close and make a profit, and then write another covered call. All of these outcomes are not only profitable but often yield double-digit returns.

A dedicated stock investor who is opposed to covered call writing will argue that when stock values rise significantly, you lose out. This is true.

EXAMPLE

If a $50 stock is exercised at $55 per share because you wrote a covered call with a 55 strike price, you gain 5 points. But what if the stock had risen to $60, $65, or even $70? The lost opportunity applies only in those situations where the price per share exceeds the sum of the strike price plus your premium income. If you sold a 55 call and received a premium of 4 ($400), you are ahead of the stock investor as long as the stock is at or below $59 per share ($55 plus $4).

The anti–covered call argument ignores the reality: Such increases in stock prices are more rare than common. You might have an occasional 100 shares called away, but for most of your stocks, the income you earn from writing covered calls is going to exceed the typical return. If a stock's price does rise, you face a dilemma: When should you sell? Do you take your profits now or hold for the long term? Covered call writing creates three advantages:

1. It discounts your basis, providing downside protection if the stock's price does decline.

2. It serves as a means for profit-taking following a price run-up without needing to sell shares.

3. Whether your covered call is exercised, expired, or closed at a profit, you increase your income.

Another point often ignored in the anti–covered call argument is the ease with which you can avoid exercise. By rolling forward and up, you create *additional* income, and you avoid exercise by replacing the current strike price with a higher one. If the rolled call is exercised, you gain more income because of the higher strike price. You can also roll forward and up indefinitely to track a rising stock. Would it be preferable to simply wait and hope all of your stocks rise? The likelihood is that some of the companies in your portfolio will take longer than others to appreciate. These are the ideal stocks for covered call writing, even with the lost opportunity risk.

A point to remember about lost opportunity: It is going to be the exception rather than the rule. When discussing speculation in long options, you will recall that about 75 percent of all options expire worthless. This means that they are not exercised, either because they fail to move in the money before expiration or they are closed before exercise occurs. So the likelihood of lost opportunity applies at the most to less than one-fourth of your portfolio, even if you were to write covered calls on all of your holdings.

Covered call writing also provides you with downside protection, which can be thought of as a way to counteract lost opportunity risk. When the stock market experiences a major correction, covered call writers can take their short call profits.

EXAMPLE

When the market fell more than 400 points in February 2007, prices rebounded quickly and new records were set for several months running. But the day after the drop in the DJIA, covered call writers were able to buy to close positions previously opened. So a drop in the level of stock prices was accompanied by drops in option premium values as well. The astute covered call writer would take advantage of a short-term correction by closing profitable positions (remember, with covered calls you sell to open and buy to close), buying positions at lower levels than they were opened. Then, when prices return to previous levels, those same covered calls (or different ones) can be resold and reopened. So lost opportunity may easily be offset by downside protection. The chances of the market

falling 400 or 500 points in one day are at least as likely as
the chances that the index will rise 400 or 500 points.

■   **Diversifying for Maximum Effect**

Everyone deals with the double problems of managing risk
and effectively diversifying. In fact, the concept of diversification is a reflection of market risk as well as each individual's perception of risk tolerance. If you diversify too
much, you spread both risk and profit potential, ending up
with a low overall rate of return. When taxes and inflation
are brought into the equation, that is not acceptable.

How do you find the right balance between beating the
tax/inflation problem and still keeping risk at a manageable level? Most people try to solve this puzzle by search-
ing for high-yielding investments that are somehow not
too risky. This is a difficult chore. An alternative is to employ options as an offset to your portfolio, reducing risk
while increasing income *without* added risk. Thus, a well-
diversified portfolio is desired but can still be used to create current income beyond dividends.

Your own perceptions of how to best diversify may include the following points:

- *Invest in value companies in* different *industries.* These
  industries must also be subject to different cyclical
  forces.

- *Remember to allocate beyond the stock market.* Some
  investors overlook the existence of markets beyond
  stocks. It is true that the stock market is exciting, easy
  to engage in, and potentially quite profitable. But other
  markets should be kept in mind in your overall financial plan. If you own your own home, you are already

allocated into real estate, and chances are your equity is the highest percentage of your overall holdings. You can also increase real estate through ETFs (Exchange-Traded Funds), real estate company stocks, and mortgage pools. If you want some funds in the bond market, bond mutual funds are probably the most realistic alternative. And some portion of your overall funds should be kept in the money market, so that you have a degree of liquidity.

- *Make sure your stock portfolio is what you want and need; sell stocks that do not fit, and replace them with ones that do.* It is very difficult to sell stocks with paper losses, because recognizing loss is painful. So there is a tendency to hold onto losing stocks hoping that their value will return. But if a company is not right for you and is not a good match for your goals, you are better off getting rid of it now and revamping your portfolio so that *all* of the holdings are good matches for you. If you diversify among appropriate and inappropriate stocks, it is not an effective method.

- *Write covered calls with strike prices above your original basis.* Once you have your portfolio set exactly as you want, you can begin using options to protect positions and to increase current income. In writing covered calls (the most profitable and least risky strategy), you should select strike prices above your original basis. By doing this, you ensure that if the short call is exercised, you will profit in three ways (dividend income, call premium, and capital gain).

- *Manage your stock and covered call portfolio carefully.* Once you have picked your stocks, you also need to manage your portfolio. Companies change and so do your goals, so today's perfect match might not be so perfect next year. You need to be willing to replace stocks as corporate financial pictures change and as your financial goals change.

When you include options as a strategic application within your portfolio, you also need to manage positions. In fact, options require more regular maintenance than value stocks. Some value investors suggest buying high-quality companies and then forgetting about them for several years. Warren Buffett recommended, "Only buy something that you'd be perfectly happy to hold if the market shut down for ten years." However, when you hold value companies and write covered calls, you need to do more management. With covered calls, you can take profits when stock (and option) values fall in the short terms, and you can roll forward to avoid exercise when stock (and option) values rise.

Diversification for its own sake makes no sense. Wider diversification is not always more effective, because it builds in only an average outcome and, in fact, programs winners *and* losers into the mix. You are far better off buying three or four exceptional companies than you are buying 20 or 30 with a mix from high to low value.

▨ Diversification Methods

The traditional and best-known form of diversification is to own many different stocks. This concept led to the widespread popularity of traditional mutual funds over the last few decades of the 20th century. But for many observers, mutual fund performance has been disappointing, perhaps because the very broad diversification practiced by funds ensures disappointing overall performance. Were it not for reinvestment of earnings, funds would not be able to report exceptional performance at all.

EXAMPLE

Everyone has read that over many decades, funds have performed well. You have probably seen statements like, "If you had invested $10,000 in 1955 and reinvested all earnings, that initial investment would be worth $71,000 in 2005." That is impressive, but on a compounded return basis, it averages only 4 percent per year—not impressive at all and far below the breakeven point with taxes and inflation.

The traditional form of diversification—owning many different stocks—is not by itself always effective. It makes more sense to diversify with only a few stocks in very different sectors. You want to avoid having too many companies in sectors subject to the same economic forces, because a downturn means that all similar sectors will be affected in the same way.

Allocating your financial assets among stocks, real estate, bonds, and the money market is sensible as well and should be done based on your individual perceptions and goals. The many online sites that recommend specific percentages to be allocated into each market are useless, because such recommendations assume all investors are the same.

Another way to diversify is by strategy, and this is where the whole portfolio management task becomes interesting. Most people agree that within the stock market, going long (buying stock) is the most popular and safest method. Shorting stock is not only expensive; it is also exceptionally risky. If a stock's value rises instead of falling, shorting stock could be quite costly. This is why it makes more sense to buy puts instead of shorting stock, for several reasons. Puts are cheaper and the maximum risk is limited to the premium cost. Some will argue that puts expire and that this is a major disadvantage. However, most people who short stock are not thinking about the long term; they expect prices to fall fairly quickly. Considering the margin cost of shorting (you have to pay interest on the stock you borrow), it is unlikely that holding short stock for many years would ever make sense.

That is one example of how options can be used to diversify, and with lower risk. Another example is the basic covered call. You are not likely to find a similar strategy offering the high returns with the low risks of covered calls. This strategy is popular because it is a sound alternative to replacing safe value stocks with more volatile issues that potentially could be more profitable. Those volatile stocks are just as likely to decline in price as they are to rise. So if you are seeking ways to diversify to increase portfolio income, using covered calls in place of higher-risk stocks just makes sense.

In Chapter 10, some long-term planning guidelines are offered with options in mind. The concepts of diversification and risk management are keys to sound management of your investment capital. Options do not have to increase risks; in fact, they can be used as a means of reducing your risk exposure.

A LONG-TERM PORTFOLIO
PLANNING GUIDE

"When we are planning for posterity, we ought to remember that virtue is not hereditary."
—Thomas Paine, *Common Sense*, 1776

N O ONE CAN ANTICIPATE every change in the market. The timing of decisions, even more than effective stock selection, often makes the difference between spectacular profits and a long waiting period. However, even when timing is off, the adage that "the market rewards patience" is worth remembering.

This book has presented a series of option strategies designed to provide you with alternatives to the buy-and-hold approach to portfolio management. There is nothing wrong with buy-and-hold, of course; it is the process most investors have applied for many decades. If you apply the principles of value investing (buying high-quality companies at bargain prices and keeping stock for the long term), you are likely to outperform the market as a whole. Options are useful for offsetting the occasional timing error *and* for taking profits without selling stock. The most popular and safest of all strategies, covered call writing, can also vastly improve year-to-year profits.

The primary point concerning the use of options is that you can use a wide range of strategies involving options and depending on the market conditions of the moment. Your option strategies work in all market conditions, including bullish run-up periods as well as multi-hundred–point drops in major corrections. It is a mistake to use one strategy in all circumstances, and it makes much more sense to have a variety of strategies available to put into action when the time is right.

In this final chapter, some closing thoughts and proposed guidelines are offered to ensure that your long-term goals and risk tolerance rule your portfolio decisions; that stock selection remains true to your perceptions of how much risk is appropriate; and that options are used only as a strategic enhancement to your present portfolio decisions.

Three Rules for Stock Selection

In Chapter 1, three rules were proposed for stock selection. In this section, these rules are repeated and expanded upon with option strategies, limitations, and opportunities in mind.

Rule #1: Pick stocks based on your well-defined objectives and risk tolerance levels, and never based on potential gains from options. This rule is perhaps the most important of all. So many investors discover options and allow themselves to become distracted, picking stocks to write covered calls in direct opposition to their own risk profile. The most volatile stocks tend to offer the richest option premium. That high income is a reflection of volatility, but if you want value stocks, you also need to avoid making this common mistake.

This does not mean that even value stocks cannot be quite profitable in terms of options. Many high-rated stocks (by Standard & Poor's Stock Reports, for example) also have attractive option pricing. So how do you know when you are picking the wrong stocks for your portfolio? One reliable answer is the P/E ratio. By limiting your selection to those stocks with P/E below a specified level, you can avoid many overpriced or volatile stocks.

EXAMPLE

You might set a rule for yourself that any stocks you purchase must have current P/E at or below 20. Look at the long-term P/E trend and check the range of reported P/E; this is important because this ratio is an oddity. It compares the current price to the latest reported earnings (which might be quite out of date). In order to get a reliable matching, you need to look at multiyear P/E trends. By setting a limitation on P/E levels, you will be able to avoid high-priced stocks. This often also means that you can avoid unusually volatile issues as well.

Rule #2: Be sure the stocks you hold are appropriate for you, and when that is no longer true, sell and replace those shares. One of the flaws in the theory of value investing is the tendency to hold for the long term no matter what. This means buying stock and forgetting about it. However, things change and these changes might also affect your judgment about whether or not you want to hold onto the stock.

EXAMPLE

If you own stock in the energy sector, what happens if a cheap alternative fuel is developed? Is your company a major player, or has it missed the trend? Or if you have invested in the retail sector, you have to realize that changes in management, number of stores, or products being offered can drastically change competitive position between two or more leading companies. You need to track companies and their fundamentals to make sure that today's fundamentals remain true in the future. When things change, it is time to get out. This often means buying today's competitive leader and holding shares until a new company takes over the dominant position in the industry (or when the trend points to this occurring).

Another factor that will affect the companies you want to own are mergers and acquisitions and the opposite, the divestiture of operating segments.

EXAMPLE

Early in 2007, Altria (formerly Philip Morris) sold off its interest in Kraft Foods and compensated stockholders with shares of Kraft. If you had been an owner of Altria prior to this time, you might have liked the diversification within this very well-managed company—but you might not want Altria now as solely a tobacco industry play. (You might also not want to own Kraft shares, incidentally.) In short, your perceptions of a company's value should be reevaluated when important changes occur.

Rule #3: Select stocks based on your belief about long-term price appreciation, above all other considera-

tions. You should never buy shares of stock primarily because you want to write covered calls or take up any other option plays. That is decision making in reverse order. You should always buy shares in companies meeting your long-term criteria and based on strong fundamentals (revenue and earnings, capitalization, dividend, P/E, excellent management, leading competitive position). The great pitfall to becoming attracted to options is that it is all too easy to overlook this basic requirement. It does you no good to make a lot of short-term profit on options only to end up with a portfolio of losing stocks. The long-term growth potential of the companies you pick should always be your primary focus; options are a strategy within your portfolio, not a replacement for good decisions.

The same rule may be applied even when you use options without owning shares. For example, if you want to swing trade, the stocks you pick should be moderately volatile and you should trade within price channels. But swing trading requires a degree of order in the trading trend, and this usually is associated with exceptionally well-managed companies. If a stock's price trend is erratic and unpredictable, swing trading is not going to work well, and the reliability of the system will break down if and when the market goes through a large change in price (for example, when the DJIA rises or falls more than 100 points in one day). Short-term volatility is a good thing, especially for swing traders, with one very important qualification: The company has to be stable enough so that short-term trends follow the "normal" rules most of the time. This means that three- to five-day trends are likely to act in a repetitive and predictable manner. By definition, highly volatile stocks do not conform to expectations in trading patterns but tend to display very erratic and unpredictable price movement.

If you keep these guidelines in mind, your use of options will likely succeed. The primary point is that options provide you with a strategic advantage for taking profits, speculating on short-term price declines, or providing downside protection (through covered calls or insurance puts, for example). Options cannot replace a sound stock selection policy, and those who have tried to use options in place of solid fundamentals have usually ended up losing rather than winning.

Seven Strategies for Option Activity

A review of the most sensible option strategies in the context of portfolio management should be a continual process. It is so easy to become distracted that a few reminders of how you can use options will help you to avoid problems.

Assuming that you believe in the fundamentals and seek long-term value companies, limit your option activity to these seven strategies:

1. *Covered call writing.* The most conservative and highest-yielding strategy is covered call writing. As previously discussed, double-digit returns are not only possible but likely. Choosing a strike price to guarantee a capital gain in the event of exercise provides overall profits from three sources: stock capital gains, dividends, and option premium. When stock prices fall, short calls can be closed at a profit; when stock prices rise above the strike price, covered calls can be closed and rolled forward and up. Even though you might occasionally have stock called away below current market value, it is possible to avoid exercise in most cases. Time works against long option traders, but when you write covered calls, deteriorating time value is the source for consistent profits. Because 75

percent of all options expire worthless, writing covered calls will be likely to produce profitable outcomes 75 percent of the time.

2. *Contingent purchase with long calls.* At times, you would like to buy additional shares of a stock you have in your portfolio, but funds are simply not available. You believe you are going to miss profits by not being able to buy now. In this situation, you can use long-term long calls to tie in the price for future purchase. This is not the same as mere speculation, assuming you want to buy shares in the future. If the stock's value remains below the strike price, your long calls expire worthless and your maximum risk is limited to the premium you paid. Considering that you lock in a strike price with the long call, the potential loss may be well worth the possibility of a limited loss.

3. *Contingent purchase with short puts.* The concept of contingent purchase is more interesting when you write short puts. In this situation, you receive premium instead of paying it. This has the effect of setting your likely basis in the stock at the put's strike price less the premium you receive. If the stock's value falls and the put goes in the money, you can avoid exercise by rolling forward and down. This strategy should be used only when you would be happy to buy additional shares at the strike price.

When short puts are exercised, you are required to pay the strike price, which will be higher than current market value. Your paper loss will equal this difference, minus the premium you received. To recover the net loss, you can write covered calls. So the strategy—even involving uncovered puts—is far less risky than writing uncovered calls.

4. *Combined covered call and uncovered put strategy.* The short spread or short straddle—employing the combi-

nation of covered call and uncovered put—is intriguing because it invariably produces an exceptionally high rate of return. The covered call is conservative because exercise produces a profit; the uncovered put is partially protected by the total premium receipts, and exercise can be avoided with rolling forward and down. If and when the put is exercised, the paper loss is recoverable through subsequent covered call writing (or doubling up of the same strategy).

One possible outcome is especially interesting. It is possible that—as a result of movement of the stock's price above the call strike *and*, at a different time, below the put's strike—both options will be exercised. As long as the call and put have identical strike prices, the buy/sell is a wash and you profit from total option income. In that case, you end up with the same position you began with. (For example, if you own 100 shares, they are called away upon exercise of the covered call; when the uncovered put is exercised, you are required to buy 100 shares. The net outcome is ownership of 100 shares and profit by way of the call and put premium.)

5. *Puts used to insure paper profits.* If you have a paper profit, you face a very common dilemma. You would like to take profits but you don't want to sell stock. In order to insure those paper profits, buying a put achieves your goal. If the stock's price falls, the decline will be matched by increases in the put's value. Thus, lost profits can be replaced by selling the appreciated put.

The limited premium cost of the put is often worth the insurance this provides. When puts are especially affordable, you may also buy *more* puts to produce extra profits. For example, if you own 200 shares and you write three puts, once they go in the money, the intrinsic value of the puts grows by 3 points for every point decline in the stock's value.

6. *Long calls to take advantage of price declines.* A form of swing trading limited to only extreme price movement often produces handsome profits. For example, whenever the index-based market value falls substantially over a one- to two-day period, it is usually an overreaction to the underlying cause. At such times, stock prices tend to fall many points. Many stock investors sell when this happens, fearing further declines—but this is a mistake. If you have picked high-quality companies, those share prices will return to previous levels. So instead of selling stock, it makes more sense to buy calls. Then, when the price does rebound, you can exercise the calls and buy more shares below market value; or you can sell the calls at their appreciated value and keep the profits.

7. *Long puts to take advantage of price acceleration.* The same swing trading approach applies when stock prices rise quickly. Just as price declines tend to be overreactions, so do rapid increases in index-based prices. So when a stock's price rises many points in a single day, buying puts is a way to swing trade on the overreaction. When prices retreat, the puts can be exercised and shares of stock sold above market value, or the puts can be sold at a profit.

This strategy is not quite the same as buying puts for insurance, even though the outcome is the same. With the insurance strategy, your purpose is to protect paper profits. When you swing trade using puts at the top of a price trend, you are trying to time the purchase to create very short-term profits in addition to the stock positions in your portfolio.

Common Mistakes Worth Avoiding

Every investor has made mistakes in decisions concerning companies to buy and in the timing of trades. This is inevitable. Any system promising to give you 100 percent profits should be doubted, because no one can profit in each and every trade. If you can beat the averages, you're well ahead of the game. This is where options give you the edge.

Even with options as part of your profitable portfolio strategy, it is always possible to make some of the common investment mistakes. These include:

- *Making decisions out of impatience.* Time perceptions among investors are often distorted. A few days seem like an eternity when a stock's price is not moving very much, or when it is slipping instead of soaring day by day. In this environment, it is easy to become impatient and make ill-advised decisions.

EXAMPLE

If you bought stock at $50 and it slipped to $47 over a one-week period, you might decide to sell and look for a company whose stock is more active. This is a mistake; a few trading days is not a long enough period to judge a company's market performance. If you select companies wisely in the first place, a short-term price decline is not a problem. Patient investors do better than impatient ones.

- When it comes to options, impatience can also lead to poor decisions. You might buy stock with the intention of writing covered calls. Ideally, the stock's price rises a few points and you can write calls with strike prices well above original basis. But when this doesn't happen quickly enough, it is tempting to write calls anyway, just to get into the action. This is also a big mistake.

Just as you want to avoid reacting to short-term price changes emotionally, effective portfolio management requires that you keep a cool head and patiently wait out price trends—both in stock and option values.

- *Selling the* wrong *covered call.* When you sell a covered call, the strike price should always be based on three factors. First is your original basis, which should be below the strike price (so that in the event of exercise, you will have a capital gain and not a capital loss). Second is proximity of current market value to strike price (if you write what the IRS defines as an "unqualified" covered call, you may lose long-term capital gain status on your stock). Third is the attribute mix of the option (premium level, difference between strike price and current market value, and time to expiration).

  The "wrong" covered call can result in loss of long-term status or programs in a net capital loss.

EXAMPLE

If you bought stock at $50 per share and its value recently slipped to $47, does writing a 45 call make sense? Even if you get a premium of 4 ($500), this is the wrong call to sell. In the event of exercise, your stock will be called away at $45 per share, which is $500 below your original basis. If you get only $400 for selling the call, you lose $100. It is not a smart move. Also, chances are better than average that the call will be exercised since it is in the money.

- *Becoming attracted to speculating in options.* Some investors, even moderate to conservative ones, discover options and allow their enthusiasm to get the best of them. Instead of staying true to their original personal

goals and trading within their well-defined risk tolerance, they begin speculating, buying calls and puts in
the hope of making a fast profit. Remember, 75 percent of all options expire worthless, so speculating in
long options is more likely—by three to one—to create
losses than profits.

The temptation is there, without doubt. The truly
effective option strategy is one that remains focused on
the short list of profitable strategies and avoids speculative moves. If you are able to avoid the temptation to
speculate, you will be able to keep more of your money
in the long run. There are conditions where buying
long options, even as a speculative move, is appropriate.

EXAMPLE

If you decide to dedicate a small portion of your capital to
swing trading, which is speculative, you are at least employing a programmed trading pattern to time your decisions. It is important, however, to avoid putting too much
capital into such ventures if you consider yourself conservative, because any sudden and unexpected change in
market conditions can wipe out your speculative long positions in a single trading day.

- *Rolling forward and creating losses instead of profits.*
  The suggestion that you can avoid exercise of short
  calls by rolling forward and up (or short puts by rolling
  forward and down) is sensible and effective—assuming it is done properly. Some investors deceive themselves, however, by creating net losses rather than
  profits. The ideal roll achieves two things. First, the existing short position is replaced by another with a different strike price (higher for calls, lower for puts).

Second, the roll creates a net breakeven or credit. This is not always possible, so a compromise is often appropriate. For example, you may roll forward to a later-expiring option with the same strike price. This creates net cash income and defers the likelihood of exercise (but does not entirely remove the possibility of early exercise, which can occur any time the option is in the money).

The mistake occurs when you make a trade-off between strike price and market value.

EXAMPLE

You buy stock at $50 per share and sell a 50 call for 2.50. Near expiration, the stock has risen to $52 per share. So you close the original short call and replace it with a later-expiring 52.50 call. However, this transaction results in a debit. You close the existing call for 4 and open the new one for 2, paying a net of $200. The justification is found in the exchange of a 50 strike for a 52.50 strike. In the event of exercise, you will gain $250 more with the higher strike. The fact that you exchange an in-the-money short call for an out-of-the-money, later-expiring short call makes sense; however, if you practice this kind of forward roll, you also need to adjust the real basis in the short position. You sold the original short call for 2.50 and closed in at 4, creating a net loss of 1.50 ($150). You opened the new position for 2 ($200), so your true basis in the short position is only $50. Considering that your 100 shares are on the line in this case, you could end up with a loss. For example, if the new call fell from 2 down to 1 and you decided to close it, what is your profit? If you look only at the rolled position, it looks like you made $100 (sold for 2, bought for 1). But because your real basis is only $50, you actually *lose* $50 on this transaction:

Sold original call	$250
Bought to close	− 400
loss	− 150
Sold rolled call	200
adjusted basis	$ 50
Bought to close	− 100
net loss	$ − 50

If this call fell in value, it also meant that the stock's market value declined. So your actual basis in the stock has to be taken up to $50.50 per share (original cost plus loss on the short call). How does this compare to current market value? Chances are good that you will have made no profit at all. In this type of transaction, you would have been better off waiting to write a call with a higher strike, and rolling forward only if it became possible to create a net credit. If those conditions were not present, it would have made sense to simply wait and accept exercise.

- *Ignoring puts and using only calls no matter what market conditions prevail.* Investors are for the most part optimists. They subscribe to the belief that the future is "that period of time in which our affairs prosper, our friends are true and our happiness is assured" (in the words of writer Ambrose Bierce).

  Of course, this belief has many blind spots, especially in investing. For example, when people buy a company's stock, they almost always consider the purchase price as a starting point and believe that prices will rise without fail. In reality, a price is part of a continuum of ever-changing buy and sell pressures and part of a trading range. The price might rise and it might fall. The same problem is seen in the options market, in the way that people trade. There is a tendency to track calls and to ignore puts. After all, if you buy a put, you are speculating that a stock's price will fall and, for many, this possibility is unthinkable. So those going long tend to buy calls most of the time. However, some market conditions make buying puts a wiser and better-timed move.

The same problem works in reverse. Those who are permanently bearish about the market will tend to *always* buy puts or, for the higher-risk group, short stock. Even during periods of long-term bull markets, there is always a group believing that the whole thing is about to come crashing down. They tend to be at least as inflexible as the more common eternal optimists. Both sides have an expensive blind spot in the inflexibility of their positions. It makes much more sense strategically to recognize that you can profit in all kinds of markets, especially using options, if you recognize the signs.

When Markets Correct

Stock market optimists thrive as long as prices rise. One problem in strong bull markets is the tendency to believe the run-up will never end. But eventually, it always does.

The history of the stock market is a history of experts and professionals being taken completely by surprise. A price correction, even a large one, is rarely anticipated by those experts. This is why big corrections are given names like "Black Monday" and the "Panic of 1907." These corrections are dire and expensive, even though the markets eventually recover. Just as bull markets end, so do bear markets. Just as run-ups correct, price declines invariably lead to a price rebound.

The realization of these market facts of life can be extremely profitable to you if you use options in your portfo-

lio, both at the point of correction and afterward. For the
covered call writer (the most likely strategy you will employ), there are two strategic moves to make after a correction. By definition, this is a large price drop in a one-
day or two-day period. Remember, markets always overreact to everything, so when prices fall hundreds of points,
it usually means the drop will correct and reverse in the
very near future. As measured by the Dow Jones Industrial
Average, many drops of more than 400 points have occurred and will occur in the future. The higher the index
moves, the bigger these corrections are likely to be. In
1929, trading over 6 million shares was considered high
volume. Today, that is nothing. The October 1929 crash,
when more than 654 percent of market value was lost
(from a Dow Jones Industrial Average level of 400 down
to a low of 145 in a single month), was certainly a disaster.
But the DJIA fell only 255 points during the month of the
crash, a larger percentage drop but a smaller point drop
than the 508 points lost in October 1987. A 400-point correct in February 2007 was relatively benign with the DJIA
above 12,000. So one-day to one-week corrections are
common, and the severity cannot be measured solely in
terms of points or percentages. For every investor, the real
effect is how the stocks in your portfolio are affected.

When a crash does occur and your stocks lose market
value, it is a two-part opportunity for everyone who keeps
a cooler head. First, you can buy-to-close all the short calls
in your portfolio, because as stock values fall, so do call
values. Second, given the likelihood that prices are going
to rebound rapidly, the post-decline fall is a good time to
buy calls at bargain prices. You will be able to find cheap
calls with strikes higher than current stock values, but
lower than pre-crash price levels. This is the profit zone
for contrarian call buying because it is probable that prices

are going to recover. In February 2007, for example, a full recovery occurred within a matter of weeks.

As an alternative to buying calls, you can also sell puts. This creates a net credit, with money coming to you rather than being paid out. As prices rise, those puts lose value and can be closed at a profit. After a big crash, many investors are fearful that the declines will continue. If, in fact, the price drop is the beginning of a long-term bear market, selling puts could be a high-risk venture. But whether you buy calls or sell puts, the correction is an opportunity to make a profit in the market. One important point to always keep in mind: If you have picked value stocks in your portfolio, prices are going to rebound, even if the market as a whole stays weak for an extended period of time. By definition, value investing restricts stock positions to companies with superior financial strength, strong competitive position in their sectors, and exceptional management. The averages are just that, and you cannot rely on the DJIA to judge the strength of any one company. If your portfolio includes value companies, they will not follow a downward trend for long. Short term, all prices are going to overreact, and in a correction that means a loss of value. But when the dust settles, the companies with strong fundamentals hold their value and, by the same rationale, overpriced companies with high P/E and weak fundamentals will tend to fall harder and stay lower than the average.

The two-part correction strategy (selling open short calls and then buying long calls) requires that you remain calm when other people are in a panic. Whenever a big correction happens, you are going to hear that it is the start of a bear market. Whenever prices rise, you also hear that stocks are overvalued. These are typical forecasts, and they are usually wrong or poorly timed. As long as you pick value companies and buy their stock, stay within your risk tolerance levels, and use options to take advantage of the overreaction of the correction itself, you will not suffer as much as those investors who react in panic and greed—selling low and buying high.

An Eye on Value Stocks

As an investor using options to trade and profit strategically (as part of a larger portfolio plan rather than as a primary effort), you always need to decide what risk levels are appropriate for you. Most people, upon studying the attributes of value companies, define themselves as value investors. This means buying high-quality stocks in well-managed, competitively dominant companies, at bargain prices—and holding those shares for the long term. It makes sense because, no matter what the indices do from year to year, value companies grow over the long term. Short-term price movement really doesn't matter . . . unless you want to take advantage of the chaotic nature of prices through option trading.

Within the narrow but efficient confines of a short list of value companies, option trading does improve overall returns.

EXAMPLE

Just holding high-value companies might produce yields of 4 percent to 8 percent over the years, especially if you reinvest dividends. But using options (especially writing covered calls) can be reasonably expected to double your returns from your portfolio. This assumes that you sell well-picked calls to ensure capital gains in the event of exercise, that you are willing to accept exercise as one possible outcome, and that you thoroughly understand the transaction. Covered call writing is a safe and conservative strategy that often results in double-digit returns no matter what the outcome.

In holding value company stocks and using various option strategies, you may also seek stocks meeting some very basic criteria:

- Look for P/E ratios within a reasonable level (for example, between 10 and 20).

- Focus on companies paying better than average dividends.

- Search among those companies that have increased the dividend for ten years or more (see Mergent's list of "Dividend Achievers" at www.dividendachievers.com).

- Restrict option activity to the conservative strategies and avoid outright speculation.

As long as you are aware of the limitations of any kind of speculative activity, you can make profitable use of options and use the power of these interesting tools to improve your overall income. There are very few other ways to create double-digit returns in your portfolio without significantly increasing your risks at the same time.

GLOSSARY

annualized return   The rate of return calculated as though investments were held for exactly one year. To calculate, divide the holding period by the months the investment was open, and then multiply the result by 12.

anti-straddle rule   A federal tax regulation that suspends long-term tax rates on the sale of stock, when the investor sells unqualified in-the-money covered calls.

assignment   Exercise against a seller, done based on orderly procedures employed by the Options Clearing Corporation and by brokerage firms.

at the money   Status on an option when the stock's value is the same as the option's strike price.

automatic exercise   The exercise of an in-the-money option that has not already been exercised or canceled, normally occurring on the last trading day.

bear spread   The purchase and sale of options to produce profits when the value of the underlying stock declines.

box spread   A combined bull spread and bear spread, opened at the same time on the same underlying stock.

bull spread   The purchase and sale of options to produce profits when the value of the underlying stock rises.

butterfly spread   Open options in one strike price range, combined with open options at both higher and lower price ranges.

calendar spread   The purchase or sale of options on the same stock, but with different expiration dates.

call   An option to buy 100 shares of stock at a fixed price.

called away   Having stock assigned, so that 100 shares of stock are called away from the owner at the strike price.

class   All options traded on a specific stock.

collar   The combination of long stock, a covered call, and a long put, when both options are out of the money.

combination   Any option transaction on one stock, with differing terms.

condor spread   A butterfly spread with different short position strike prices above or below the middle range.

contract   The agreement between buyer and seller in an option. Identification of the stock, the option cost, the date of expiration, and the strike price are involved.

cover   Owning 100 shares of a stock when a call is sold.

covered call   A call sold short, when the seller owns 100 shares of stock.

credit spread Any spread creating higher premium income than cost.

current market value The market value of stock or of options.

debit spread Any spread creating lower premium income than cost.

deep in the money Status of options more than 5 points above the strike price of the call or below the strike price of the put.

deep out of the money Status of options more than 5 points below the strike price of the call or above the strike price of the put.

diagonal spread A calendar spread with both long and short positions containing different strike prices and expiration dates.

exercise Buying stock under the terms of the call or selling stock under the terms of the put.

expiration date The date when options becomes worthless, specified in the option contract.

expiration time The latest possible time to place an order on an option on the last trading day.

extrinsic value The non-intrinsic premium of options not specifically related to time; a reflection of perceived stock volatility and potential for profit.

hedge The use of one position to offset another, such as options used to protect stock positions.

horizontal spread A calendar spread with offsetting long and short positions, containing identical strike prices but different expiration dates.

in the money Of a call when the stock's market value is higher than the option's strike price, or of a put when the stock's market value is lower than the option's strike price.

intrinsic value An option's current value equal to the points that it is in the money.

last trading day The Friday before the third Saturday of the expiration month.

LEAPS Long-Term Equity Anticipation Securities, long-term option contracts.

long hedge Using options to insure a stock position in case of a price increase; or used by short sellers needing insurance against the risk of a rise in the stock's price.

long position A buy order placed in advance of entering a sell order, and closed by later entering a sell order, or by expiration of the option.

long straddle Buying the same number of options with the same strike prices and expiration dates.

married put A put used to hedge a long stock position. If the stock value falls, the put's value rises to offset the loss.

naked option A call sold when the seller does not own 100 shares of the stock.

offsetting positions A federal tax distinction, a straddle that creates a reduction in risk; when positions are called offsetting, investors may lose deductibility of losses or long-term gains tax rates.

option A contract providing the buyer rights to buy or to sell 100 shares of stock at a fixed price on or before a future date, after which the option is worthless.

out of the money Of a call when the stock's market value is lower than the option's strike price, or of a put when the stock's market value is higher than the option's strike price.

paper profits Values found only on paper but not taken at the time, which are realized only if those positions are closed.

premium The price of an option, with the amount expressed without dollar signs but as single numerals.

put An option to sell 100 shares of stock at a fixed price.

put to seller The exercise of a put, when the seller has to buy 100 shares of stock at the strike price.

qualified covered call A covered call meeting tax law requirements that allow long-term gain rates to apply, or to keep the long-term holding period in effect; determined by the time to expiration, and by the price levels between market value of the stock and strike price of the call.

ratio calendar combination spread Both a ratio between purchases and sales and a box spread. Long and short positions are opened on the same stock, with expiration dates extending over two or more dates.

ratio calendar spread   A different number of long and short options, when expiration dates are also different.

ratio write   Covering of one position only partially.

return if exercised   The rate of return option sellers earn if the call is exercised, including profit or loss from the sale of stock, dividend income, and option premium.

return if unchanged   The rate of return option sellers earn if the call is not exercised, including dividends earned and option premium.

reverse hedge   Long or short hedge when more options are opened than the number needed to cover, increasing profit when unfavorable price change occurs in the stock.

rolling forward   Replacement of one written call with another that expires later or has a different strike price.

seller   The person granting an option right to a buyer, who also profits if the stock moves below the price (call) or above the price (put) of stock.

short hedge   Purchase of options to insure a portfolio position in case of a price decline, or to protect long positions with insurance in the event of a market decline.

short position   Entering a sale as an opening move, and closing the position later through a buy order or upon expiration.

short selling   When shares of stock are sold, creating a short position, and later bought to close.

short straddle Selling the same number of calls and puts with the same strike prices and expiration, which creates profits only within a limited price range.

spread The purchase and sale of options on the same stock, but with different strike prices, different expirations, or both.

straddle The purchase and sale of options with the same strike prices and expirations.

strike price The price that will be paid for 100 shares, articulated in the option contract; the price per share of stock upon exercise, regardless of the market value of the stock at the time.

tax put A combined sale of stock at a loss and the sale of a put. The premium from the put offsets the loss on the stock. If the put is exercised, the stock can be bought at the strike price.

terms The striking price, expiration month, type of option (call or put), and the underlying stock.

time value An option's current premium above intrinsic value.

total return The return from selling a call, capital gain on stock, and dividends.

uncovered option The sale of an option not protected by the 100 shares of the stock.

underlying stock The stock on which options are bought or sold.

variable hedge   A hedge with a long and short position in related options, when one side contains more options than the other.

vertical spread   A spread with options having different strike prices but identical expirations.

wash sale rule   A rule in the tax code prohibiting deduction of stock losses if and when the position is reopened within 30 days from the date of the sale.

writer   The person who sells a call or a put.

INDEX